The experiences in this surprising book are drawn directly from the daily life of a New York taxicab driver in good standing. Mr. Hazard has been "hacking" the city for almost nine years.

He deals with phases of life of which the average reader knows not at all—the "rackets" a taxi man has to fight, the graft he has to pay, the characters of the half-world he meets—and much more.

The book compares "hacking" conditions to-day and ten years ago, when the author got his first license by shaking hands with an official and forgetting to remove a ten-dollar bill from the political palm when the handshaking was over. Every page is packed with human interest and keen understanding of character.

The author came to New York to "see life in Greenwich Village." Since he *had* to make a living, he thought taxi driving was as good a way as any other. He is in his thirties, was a hobo and wanderer before he was a taxi driver and is still piloting his cab through the tangles of New York traffic.

—From the original dust jacket flap

"It is refreshing to meet a realistic writer who refuses to clutter his pages with superfluous details in an effort to make his point as clear as a gun held against the ribs. Everything is done quite neatly and with dispatch, and it is surprising that, being neat, it can remain true."

—Ira Wolfert, *Books*

"'Hacking New York' is heartily recommend. It is entertaining, instructive and unfailingly readable from start to finish."
—Edward Hope, *New York Herald Tribune*

"Hazard is a born storyteller, especially for his humor and crisp simplicity, and a born raconteur. He tells a hundred vibrating experiences from that man-eating, money-crazy jungle through which New Yorkers pass every day."
—George Britt, *New York Telegram*

"Mr. Hazard has an ingenious and resourceful mind, whether in mechanical tinkering or the use of words, and he tells no end of yarns that are highly entertaining and also most instructive as to the ways of taxi drivers. The book is largely made up of stories of his own experiences with passengers and officials, and because he has a keen and genial sense of humor they are all beguiling."
—*The New York Times*

"The splendors and miseries of a taxi driver's life are well set forth in Hacking New York.'"
—W. R. Brooks, *Outlook*

"A difficult form of writing is the brief sketch, usually essayed only by adepts. Neat selection of detail, curt force of language, descriptive finesse is necessary. Taximan Hazard possesses these literary attributes."
—*Time Magazine*

HACKING NEW YORK

Robert Hazard

Introduction by Jeff Vorzimmer

INCLUDES THREE
SHORT STORIES
AND
THE ORIGINAL
SERIALIZED
PUBLICATION

Staccato
CRIME
AN IMPRINT OF STARK HOUSE PRESS

Other Titles from Staccato Crime

Dust jacket of the first edition of
Hacking New York, *1930*

Table of Contents

Introduction

The Mystery of Robert Hazard

Little is known about Robert Hazard, author of a book of anecdotes from the life of a New York City taxi cab driver, *Hacking New York,* and a few short stories, all of which were published in *Scribner's Magazine.* The few interviews he gave after the publication of his book offered scant details about his life before arriving in New York. In conversations with his fares he claimed to have come from Virginia, but in at least one instance, when a fare recognized his accent, he admitted having been born in Chicago.

Hazard claimed to have been a hobo before arriving in New York in 1921, working as a farm hand in California, a plantation foreman in Virginia, and a shipyard worker in Philadelphia before making his way north. None of it can be confirmed since there is no paper trail of his life before 1924, the first year he appears as a resident of Greenwich Village in New York City.

He told one fare that he had come to New York with literary aspirations but failed to get anything published, so started driving a taxi to pay the bills. He had been driving a cab for eight years when his luck changed. He met thirty-seven-year-old spinster librarian and Wellesley grad Marion Isabel Lord. Having worked as not only a librarian, but as an editor as well, she helped Hazard turn his humorous anecdotes of driving a cab into publishable form. She could not have helped being impressed by the intellect of this handsome, college-educated, struggling author who had traveled the country as a hobo and could play the piano beautifully. Within months of meeting her, Hazard had contributed a series of anecdotes to *Scribner's*, which were serialized in the November and December issues of 1929, and they were asking for more.

When Scribner's accepted his anecdotes for book publication, the couple made plans to marry. With their own future still uncertain, as well as that of the country itself, they married, two days after the stock market crash of 1929 on November 1 and ten days short of Marian's thirty-eighth birthday.

Hacking New York was published as a book in April 1930, and by all indications it didn't sell well. It was bad timing that Hazard was beginning his literary career just as the world was sliding into a global recession, but by 1935 the couple had accumulated enough money to realize the dream of buying a farm in rural Louisa County, Virginia. For four years they lived and worked on the farm, and then in 1939 Robert disappeared. It's not clear if Marian was aware that he had returned to driving a cab in New York City, but she herself returned to her childhood home in Athol, Massachusetts, and three years later, on July 16, 1942, she filed for divorce on the grounds of "desertion."

Back in New York City at the start of American involvement in the Second World War, at the age of 51, Hazard found that he was not too old to have to register for the draft. On April 27,1942, the draft was expanded to include 45- to 64-year-olds. It's telling that on the line of his draft registration card where he was to fill in the "Name and address of persons who will always know your address," he put the name of his lawyer in Virginia rather than the wife to whom he was still married.

With Marian living back at home with her parents, Hazard returned to Virginia and worked again as a farmer. Sometime in 1945 he got a diagnoses of lung cancer—no doubt from years of smoking cartons of unfiltered Camels—and realized he was dying. From his deathbed he made a startling confession. He was not born Robert Hazard.

When a person commits suicide, he leaves many unanswered questions. Similarly, when a person orchestrates his own disappearance, he not only leaves behind unanswered questions, but creates two mysteries in his wake—the mystery of what has become of him and the mystery of the past of the man he became. Such was the case of the man who called himself Robert Hazard.

The Mystery of Frank Scholes

Walter Francis Scholes was born in Chicago on August 5, 1890, to a middle-class couple named Thomas and Lydia. These were the only facts he had in common with the man named Robert Hazard. Walter Francis, called "Frank," was the black sheep of the family, the youngest of seven children, two of whom died in infancy. His father was a Civil War veteran who owned a company that sold school textbooks and supplies, and his mother was a physician.

Young Frank was a talented pianist with dreams of being a songwriter, but his parents pushed him toward a more practical career, and he enrolled in the University of Illinois to study agriculture. In 1913, he met Blanche Helene Walker, the daughter of a Springfield attorney and gentleman farmer, Alexander J. Walker. They were wed on July 17, 1913.

The young married couple worked one of the several farms the Walker family owned and, one day short of their first anniversary, Blanche's mother gave them a 40-acre farm of their own near the state fairgrounds, north of Springfield (Blanche's father had died just three months after their marriage).

Frank loved horses, dogs and breeding cattle. On their farm they produced corn and dairy. Just nine months after their marriage, Thomas Francis, the first of three boys, was born in May 1914, followed by Daniel Ransom in 1915 and Kenneth Neal in 1917.

By all accounts Frank was happy and content until 1917, when the U.S. entered the Great War, and in June draft registration was required of all 21- to 30-year-olds. Although, at 26, Frank was squarely in the age range, it was likely his draft status would have been IIc (temporarily deferred, but available for military service) and not likely to be called up, being not only a farmer, but having a pregnant wife and two young children dependent on him. But this didn't keep Frank from obsessing over the possibility of being drafted and sent to a foxhole to die somewhere in Europe. On his draft registration card, on the line that read, "Do you claim exemption from draft (specify grounds)?" he wrote, "Yes, I won't go."

By July 1918, there seemed to be no end in sight for the war, and the draft was expanding and would eventually include men to the age of 45. Almost daily there were stories in the local newspapers about young men sought and prosecuted for avoiding the draft. It wasn't enough to say you weren't going to go, as Frank had. They would come for you anyway. By July 6th, Frank had made a fateful decision. He went into downtown Springfield to sell a load of corn. After selling the corn he bought a new gray suit, a gray hat, a pair of shoes, and a new pair of eyeglasses with some of the proceeds of the sale. Upon returning from town, he told his wife of his intention of going for a swim in the Sangamon River near a popular campsite. He took with him the new clothes he purchased.

Frank headed two miles north to a particularly inaccessible spot on the Sangamon River between the camp site owned by William DeSilva and the Chinkapin Bridge. He got out of his car near the bank of the river and took off his clothes, which he neatly piled on the fender of his Ford Model T, along with his eyeglasses. He walked down to the bank of the river, then carefully retraced his steps backward to the car where he put on the new gray suit and shoes, hat and eyeglasses and walked away from the river never to be heard from again.

That evening, when her husband hadn't returned, Blanche called DeSilva to see if he had seen him and telling DeSilva of Frank's intention of going for an early evening swim near his camp. DeSilva offered to go down to the river to take a look and found the Ford with the clothes neatly piled on the fender with the eyeglasses on top. He began calling out for Frank, but he was nowhere in sight. He then gathered some local farmers to search and drag the river.

The first reaction of the searchers was that Frank committed suicide, even though there was no note to that effect and nothing in his actions leading up to that day to indicate that he was any way suicidal. In fact, his fear of dying on the battlefield would suggest the opposite.

There was soon a growing suspicion among law enforcement and the county coroner, Scott Walter, that the drowning had been staged. The suspicion was confirmed after interviewing two young girls whose family was staying at the DeSilva campsite. They reported seeing a man walking away from the river in different clothes, a gray suit, than he was wearing on the way in. There was also the testimony of two of Frank's friends, who claimed to have seen him at 9:00 p.m. the day he disappeared on a street car in the Lincoln Park neighborhood, just four miles south of the river.

Despite these witnesses, Blanche and family friends still believed that Frank had been swept downstream and possibly drowned. She called his older brothers, who offered to come to Springfield to help with the search effort. The river was dragged several times over the following three days, but no sign of Frank turned up. Eventually, Blanche conceded to herself that the drowning/suicide was likely a ruse to avoid the draft, although she told her three boys that their father had drowned. She must have seen the irony in the idea of a man terrified of dying on the battlefield committing suicide. For his part, Frank could justify abandoning his family as the same outcome as if he were killed on a distant battlefield.

Blanche never had Frank declared dead, perhaps in the hope he would someday return. She never remarried and soon realized after Frank's disappearance that she couldn't run the farm by herself, which she then sold to buy a grocery store. It's a testament to Blanche's fortitude that she was able to put all three of her sons through college while running a grocery store. In 1935, with all three of her boys at the University of Illinois in Urbana, she opened a grocery store there in order to be closer to them.

Tragedy struck two years later when Blanche was in Springfield visiting friends. On Saturday, April 24, 1937, a fast-moving train through downtown Springfield struck Blanche's car and killed her. She died never knowing that her husband was still alive.

A Deathbed Confession

If Robert Hazard's deathbed confession was startling to those around him, it was even more so to the three boys he had left in Illinois, who had grown up believing their father had drowned in the Sangamon River 27 years before. Hazard sent for them so that they could be by his side and allow him to make amends. They initially balked at the invitation.

The oldest, Thomas, finally acquiesced, perhaps out of a sense of obligation, but more likely because he was the closest to Virginia, living at the time in Reading, Pennsylvania, only 250 miles to the north. The second death of Frank Scholes was on December 23, 1945.

The details of the meeting between Thomas and his father are unknown, as Thomas, who was a civil engineer, would die himself just seven years later, in November 1952, when the single-engine plane he was piloting crashed into Backbone Mountain, West Virginia, near the Maryland border.

Frank Scholes would never again see his two youngest sons, Daniel, who would become a surgeon, and Kenneth, an aeronautical engineer, nor see any of his nine grandchildren.

Jeff Vorzimmer
Austin, Texas
January 22, 2024

Sources:
Daily Illinois State Journal, October 10, 1913, p 11
Daily Illinois State Journal, July 15, 1914, p 12
Daily Illinois State Register, July 6, 1918, p 2
Daily Illinois State Journal, July 6, 1918, p 5
Daily Illinois State Journal, July 7, 1918, p 12
Daily Illinois State Journal, July 8, 1918, p 4
Olean Times Hearld, November 19, 1929, p 5
New York Daily News, April 22, 1930, p 8
Cumberland Evening Times, November 28, 1952, pp 17, 28

Acknowledgements

The editor would like to thank the extraordinary Scholes family for their invaluable input and enthusiasm for this project, especially Frank Scholes' granddaughters, Caroline Blake and Rosemary Jones, who held the key to uncovering the mystery of Robert Hazard. They provided a depth and humanity to the story beyond the cold hard facts.

A whole book could be written about the Scholes family and it would be fascinating reading. Indeed, there has been a family genealogy written titled *The American Descendants of George Scholes of Accrington, Lancashire* (Heitman Publishing, 1944) with interesting anecdotes on family members. Despite the fact that the book claims to have complete information as of January 1, 1933, there is no mention of the death or disappearance of Frank Scholes, though his entry includes information on his wife and three boys.

It is perhaps a disservice to the Scholes family to write about its one black sheep. In fact, in my discussions with various family members, it became clear to me that there still exists a bitter enmity toward the memory of Frank Scholes, even a hundred years later.

During my research I couldn't help but wonder what Frank Scholes' father, a Civil War veteran, would have thought about his youngest son abandoning his family to avoid conscription during the First World War.

Thomas Jefferson Scholes had met Abraham Lincoln as a young boy and was in so in awe and so fiercely loyal to him that, though he was just 14 years old when the Civil War began, he followed the Illinois Infantry into battle as a drummer boy. He eventually enlisted and become a soldier as soon as he turned 18 in 1864, less than a year before Lincoln's assassination.

In addition to the newspapers cited in the *Sources*, information was obtained from the Departments of Health and Vital Statistics of the Commonwealth of Virginia and the State of New York, as well as from census data, World War I and World War II draft registration cards, and from the National Archives and Records Administration.

NOTHING'S ON LEVEL IN TAXI RACKET, SAYS CAB VETERAN

The front of a typical taxi meter showing the four seals placed on it in order to prevent unauthorized moving of the front cover and tampering with the adjustments. Robert Hazard, however, says it is easy to change the meters without detection.

Inspectors O. K. Doctored Meters for Favorites.

Take it from Hackman Robert Hazard, Mayor Walker's veto of the increased taxi rates won't really mean a thing to many knights of the 15-and-5's.

For just as there is more than one way to skin a cat, so are

Robert Hazard who says meter tampering is easy.

there many ways—three, in fact—to increase the pulse beats of a lagging taxi meter.

"Clock Hospitals" Thrive.

This larcenous practice is so popular, Hackman Hazard says, that a dozen "clock hospitals" in Manhattan and the Bronx thrive these days upon the trade of taxi drivers who pay to have their meters adjusted to snatch that

One of the seals on typical taxi meter.

extra nickel or dime from the purse of John W. Passenger.

Hazard has driven a cab in New York for ten years. Once he owned a fleet of them. He has worked for Larry Fay, cab mogul, and other firms. He has written a book, out today, entitled "Hacking New York."

Pointing to the meter on his Motor Cab Transportation System vehicle, Hazard laughed:

"I could fix that in twenty minutes so it would tick off twice the legal fare. Others can and do. This rate argument is the bunk, brother."

Then, There's This Way.

Hazard seized a pair of pliers. He pointed with them to two wire strands, sealed with leaden tags.

"You break those," he exclaimed, "and put in a new drive gear at the bottom of the clock. The gyp gear has more teeth than the regulation one.

"Then you press the clipped wire together with these pliers and twist it around so it won't show at an average inspection. You haven't touched the seal, you see."

Hazard took up the floor board of his cab. A cable ran from the meter to the transmission. There was another wire with a seal. He pointed out that this wire may be cut, and a worn gear, with more than the specified number of teeth, may be substituted to speed up the meter there, instead of tampering with the meter itself.

Says Nothing's on Level.

Hacks are inspected quarterly. Drivers with doctored meters have favorite inspectors, Hazard said, and they keep their cars in their districts. Otherwise they have their meters corrected before inspection.

"Nothing is on the level in this racket," Hazard commented, "so what are they all hollering about?"

New York Daily News
April 22, 1930

HACKING NEW YORK

I came to New York just to see the sights, particularly Greenwich Village, and I made some friends in the Village. About that time my money ran low and I thought I had better get something to do to live on. Hack driving seemed to be a very handy way to see New York and eat at the same time, so I talked to hack drivers about the business of getting a license. Following their instructions I first got a chauffeur's license from the State. Then I went over to the taxi License Bureau and got an application.

In the application I was supposed to put down the names of my employers for the past five years. My employers for the previous five years were scattered all over the United States and I had forgotten how many there were, so I got out a newspaper and turned to the legal notice and picked out the name of five bankrupt firms.

I had to declare whether I had ever been in jail or not and if so when, where, and how. I had been in jail once out in California along with another fellow, but we had slipped the jailer two dollars and he had locked us in a cell that some yeggs had occupied previously and they had dynamited a hole in the floor and dug a tunnel out along the sewer pipes, so we got out and caught the next train. As this left no record, I felt no uneasiness in answering the question with a "No."

The application required me to have two men in New York who owned their own business make out vouchers for me, stating they had known me so long and I was thoroughly honest and reliable, etc., and swear to them before a notary public. I went into the delicatessen store and bought about a dollar's worth of provisions and got the delicatessen dealer to make one out without having it sworn. I went into the cigar store next door, bought a carton of Camels, and got him to fill out the other one. Then I had to get my last previous employer to sign another voucher for me, swearing that I was of unblemished character and that he was eager to hire me again. I had one of the Greenwich Villagers swear he had employed me as chauffeur. Then I went back to the License Bureau, and there are a lot of notary publics located around there who will swear to anything for a quarter apiece. As I remember it, there was a dollar's worth of swearing to be done.

Next the hack drivers told me I would have to stand an examination as to knowledge of the city, all the piers, hotels, out of the way streets, etc. I would have to be finger printed and would have to leave photographs of myself, which would be investigated by the Police Department for ten days to see if I had any police record. But they also informed me that by slipping a certain man in the office ten dollars I could avoid all these formalities and get a license right away. They told me how to pick him out. I went in and spotted him all right, called him over to one side, introduced myself, and shook hands with him, with a ten in my palm. He said, "Have they got anything on you?"

I said, "Nope."

"Come back at two o'clock."

I went back at two o'clock and he had the book and badge and everything all ready for me.

About five years later when I was in there I heard them examining some applicants as to their knowledge of the city. They asked them the location of some places I don't know yet.

BREAKING INTO THE TAXI GAME

When I got my license I already had a job in sight, so I went to work the same day for a fellow who had one cab. He drove it himself in the daytime and hired me as night driver. He had a stand-in with the private cops at Grand Central and told me how to work it there, so I made my start in the height of the rush hour at Grand Central. Luckily my first call was to Penn Station, and I knew where that was anyway, but I didn't know where cars were supposed to drive in so I set him off on Eighth Avenue. Apparently he didn't know any better, either, and I got just as good a tip as one might expect.

The next call was downtown somewhere. I hadn't a notion where it was so I started off in the direction I was headed in and after going a block and a half I turned and said, "Well, now, where is that place, anyway?" They didn't want to get out after having gone that far, so they told me how to get there and I made out all right. I worked that scheme right along and didn't have any trouble, though I got into some terrible mix-ups making theatre calls—I did get some awful bawlings out from the cops in the theatre district—in fact, I made more in a way than I made after I knew the City. I got a call to Coney Island and rambled all over Brooklyn, ran up about twelve dollars on the clock and got it with a substantial tip without a whimper. I never would have the nerve to pull anything as rough as that if I had known how to get there. I never have got as much since for a trip to Coney Island.

At first I was always violating traffic regulations. I tried telling the cops that I was new at the business as an excuse for getting tangled up, but I found that didn't do any good at all. They said, "Ah, that's what they all say."

During the first two or three months I got about all the different kinds of summonses there are. However, I became pretty good at talking them out of it. If a taxi driver tells a cop that he didn't know about it or it wasn't his fault, he is sunk, he'll get a ticket sure. But if you admit that you pulled a boner or that you didn't think he was looking or something of that sort, they are very apt to let you off, because they know that we make our living on the streets day and night in all weather just the same as they do.

I got caught passing the street car on the wrong side on East Broadway and got a summons for the eight-foot law, which carries a minimum fine of twenty dollars. The cop says, "What's the matter? You ought to know better than that."

I said, "Well, we have been passing those cars on the wrong side right along; it's the only way to get by them; and I didn't know they had a cop here."

When I appeared in Traffic Court the cop had about a dozen truck drivers that he had given summonses to for not keeping close enough to the curb. This violation carries a small fine. He lined me right up with the truck drivers and the clerk of the court read off the one charge for the whole outfit, then went through the papers and said to everyone. "How do you plead?" and we all said, "Guilty, guilty, guilty" down the line. The Judge said, "Two dollars apiece," so we filed past the cashier and handed in our two bucks.

There is an ordinance that taxis are not allowed to stand except at designated hack stands. This ordinance is enforced only on special occasions in case the property owners complain or there is some particular reason. I used to stand down in front of the Customs House, which is forbidden territory, and got good business there in the daytime. The cops used to merely chase me out once in a while. One day the cop came along with a man in plain clothes. He told the cop to give me a summons for standing there. The cop stalled around and said he thought I hadn't been there very long and asked me what I was standing there for. I told him I had had a call down there and had stopped to light a cigarette. The cop was going to let me off, but the other fellow insisted on his giving me a summons.

When we got up in Traffic Court the cop said, "Say anything you want when you get up there. I tore up your record." (The Courts keep a full record of every taxicab chauffeur's summonses and disposition made of them, and it is supposed to be laid before the Judge along with each new summons.) I told the Judge the same story I had told the cop. The cop said I had been there only a minute or two. So the Judge let me off with a dollar fine.

Some hack drivers have a terrible grouch against cops, but they are usually the kind of men who never could be in the wrong, such a thing just couldn't happen. I have run into some pretty low skunks among the cops, but take them all in all, I think they are a very decent bunch of men.

The Traffic Court magistrates are very rough on taxi drivers, but I think after all they have to be. It certainly is true that a taxi driver isn't in a position to plead ignorance.

I was up in the Traffic Court for a second-offense speeding, the fine for which is fifty dollars, which I could ill afford to pay. I thought of trying to talk them out of it, but watching the cases ahead of me, it seemed as though the ones who talked got charged for it. One fellow told about how he had eight children to support and couldn't spare the money. The Judge said, "I will take all that into consideration in your case and make it as easy as I can for you. Fifty dollars or ten days." I thought I might just as well keep my mouth shut. The cop said if I wanted to plead guilty and pay the fine, I could go before another Judge and get it over quick, so I joined the procession through the Judge's private rooms.

The clerk at the door kept mumbling, "How do you plead?"

The defendants, "Guilty, guilty, guilty," as they went by.

The Judge, "Fifty dollars apiece."

The cashier took in the money and gave receipts.

Well, after all, I knew I was speeding and was figuring on not getting caught. And I expect the man with the eight children knew he was speeding too and he probably knew he had the eight children; that is, if he did actually have them.

I found a summons in the mail one morning to appear before the Commissioner of Licenses on the complaint of the New York Central. I didn't know just what it was all about. There had been about half a dozen of us who had been slipping the special cop at the entrance on Vanderbilt Avenue fifty cents a night to look the other way and give us a chance to pick up calls there. That entrance is intended for private cars and independent taxicabs to discharge passengers. In spite of the fact that the company cabs have a private entrance down on the level where the trains come in, where they have starters and signs, everything to direct the people where to get the cabs, a lot of passengers come up to that Vanderbilt Ave. entrance, so there is good business there, and they are usually good calls. On that account the company has to put a special cop there to chase the taxicabs out, because cabs discharging passengers will linger as long as possible in the hope of picking up one, thus preventing other cars from coming in. Our understanding with the cop was that we were to linger only so long and if we didn't get anything, we were to cruise around the block, then dodge in again. We all knew when the trains were breaking and how to manage it.

The cop got hungry and let a whole lot more in on the racket, and there got to be so many of us there was scarcely enough business for us and everybody was inclined to stall longer.

I went down to the License Bureau at the time specified in the summons. There was a whole crowd of hackmen who worked around Grand Central.

The Commissioner called us all into his office, closed and locked the door. "Now," he said, "you are all old timers and I can speak frankly. I know the situation there at Grand Central. We tried to have the Vanderbilt Ave. entrance declared a public hack stand and protect your rights there. We even went to court with it, but the Railroad Company owns the property, and we lost. Now, you've got me into a jam. The President of the New York Central tried to drive in there in his limousine Monday and there were so damned many taxicabs in there stalling that he couldn't get in and had to get out in the middle of the street and walk in. There has been a lot of pressure put on me to make an example of you fellows, but I'm not going to do it. I brought you up here to serve notice on you that if any of you fellows get caught stalling in there again. I'll break you. And don't come up here with any letter from any politician or with any hard luck story. This is fair warning."

TWO WOMEN AND BENNY LEONARD

I had a call to Grand Central. As I let the party out I knew there was a train breaking right then. The cop was after us, chasing the empty cabs out. I stalled, putting the money in my pocket, closing the cab door, putting the flag up, and still the people weren't coming out from the train. Just then a cab cut in in front of me, so that held me for a while. The cop tried to make me back up and get out, and while I was monkeying around, I managed to stall the motor, so I had to get out and crank it. The cop was frothing at the mouth. By the time I got back on the cab, two middle-aged women came out and wanted a taxi, so I opened the door for them, and the cop was fit to be tied. They got in. They wanted to tell me right there all about where they were going but I told them I would drive outside and they could tell me then.

I got out and pulled up at the curb and they gave me an address away up in the Bronx. They said they were going to visit their niece, who was teaching school in New York. I knew from their accent they came from the Middle West, the same as I did. They might have been my own aunts. Well, I got them clear up in the Bronx, and I found there wasn't any such number. It was away after dark; business places were closed. I tried to hunt up the woman's name in the telephone book. It wasn't there. I tried looking for the same number on streets that had similar names. Couldn't find it. Finally I called up the Board of Education. I didn't expect to find anybody there, but I did and they hunted up this woman's address from their records, so I drove to that address. The landlady said she had moved, but she had her address. I took that address, chased it down, and by golly, it was right; she was really there. Well, the two women were too pleased and grateful for anything, and one of them said, "And it's only four fifty. Isn't that reasonable." She handed me five dollars and they both thanked me. Well, sir. I just simply didn't have the heart to break the sad news to them that it was fourteen fifty on the clock. I took the five spot and thanked them, drove off, and kicked myself all the way downtown. I says to myself, "I'll certainly have to go like hell to-night to make up that ten bucks for the boss."

I ran along and ran along, picking up short calls, and figuring I would have to turn in an I. O. U. Finally I made the breaks at the fight at the Garden, and I picked up Benny Leonard and four other pugs. I took them up to 114th Street and Seventh Ave. There was two forty on the clock. Benny says, "How much is it?" and I says, "Three eighty." Benny hands me four bills. Three of them were ones and one was a ten. I thanked him but started in second.

SCOTCHMAN

You know there is something in this stuff about the peculiarities of races and nations.

I picked up a guy at 90th and Amsterdam last night and he says, "Tek me to the Caledonia Club."

"Where the hell's the Caledonia Club?" I says.

"Dinna ye ken the Caledonia Club? It's Fefty-fefth Street and Seventh Ave."

I says, "All right. Get in." I opened the door and he climbed in.

I took a look back to see how traffic was for a quick turn-around and he says, "God have mercy. There's fefteen cents already."

BUCKERS

Outsiders never seem to understand what hack drivers mean by buckers. I have never seen the term properly used in any of the newspaper articles I have read on the subject. The newspaper reporters call them "hackers," "backers," etc. As I understand it, the term came into use in this way. In the early days there were only a few places where one had a chance to get passengers, the hotels, railroad terminals, and steamer piers. There wasn't enough business to offer any good chance to pick up calls cruising. The hotel owners, etc., claimed the right to dictate who should solicit business at their doors and sold to companies the privilege of standing for calls at their doors, and for a time got away with it. The few places that were not so controlled were worked by independents, who formed groups and kept outsiders from working those stands by slugging them. Quite naturally the best fighters gravitated to the Stands, and the less capable fighters were left out. These tail enders then formed the Twentieth Century Brown & White Taxicab Owners Association and cut the rate from the previous forty cents a mile for two passengers and sixty cents for more than two to a straight thirty cents a mile. They painted their cabs brown and white so as to make them easily distinguishable. These low-rate cabs were so much in demand that they could get more business cruising the streets than the others could get on the best stands. Now, playing a line had become known as bucking a line, probably because it involved considerable trouble—one had to be able to fight, and other cab drivers were always attempting to crash (cut in in front of you)— so when cruising became profitable, the old timers, who stuck to the high rate and played the lines, became known as buckers.

Although a great many of the old, closed lines have been broken up and are at present worked by low-rate cabs, the term is still in use to designate the old timers who run at as high a rate as possible and who get the business more or less by fighting for it. They play the water front more than anything else now. Most of them belong to an association and they own their own insurance company for bonding their own cars.

The Brown and White Taxicab Association registered their color scheme as a trade mark and fought the imitators through the courts for several years, clear up to the Supreme Court, and lost. Up to the time they lost, a membership in the organization was worth over two hundred dollars, but as soon as they lost, everybody painted brown and white, and a membership was worth nothing. The Taxi License Bureau kept the buckers with the high-rate clocks from using the brown and white color simply by refusing to license them, although they hadn't a vestige of legal authority. At this time over half of the taxicabs were Fords and most of the remainder were old second-hand cars of good makes, Packards, Renaults, Lancias, Delaunay-Bellevilles, etc. A hackman with a nice new Ford was at the top of the heap.

Just as the Brown and Whites had almost wiped out the buckers, the Yellow Cab Company came into New York with a fleet of brand new Yellow cabs, and they took the business away from everybody else almost over night. Then everybody went to painting yellow in imitation, and a great many sold their old cars and bought new Yellows, as the Company operating the cabs was independent of the manufacturers.

When about half the hack drivers in the city were paying installments on new Yellow cabs, the Mogul Checker Manufacturing Company came into the City and started several fleets. Their cabs were designated by a checker stripe. They took the business away from the Yellows just about as quick as the Yellows had taken it away from the Brown and Whites. I understand that that summer the Yellow Cab Company took back over two thousand cabs whose owners were unable to make payments, and I know of a number of owners who ran for five or six months without paying any notes, simply because the Company apparently didn't have a place to put the cabs if they seized them.

Well, the Mogul Checkers had everything all their own way for the best part of two years, and finally they had sold cabs to about half the independents in town, when the old Twentieth Century Association was revived and again cut the rate, this time to twenty cents a mile. This time they painted their cabs a bright red with a stripe of white, black, and gold. Immediately they took the business away from everybody else. Mogul Checker fleet owners were going broke in every direction.

Just before the Twentieth Century cut the rate, another outfit had invaded the field—the Luxors. They went into the hands of the receivers soon after the Twentieth Century came out.

The Twentieth Century, of course, was unable to keep imitators from using their color, and in a very short time there were more imitations on the street than there were genuine Twentieth Centuries. More money was being made at twenty cents a mile than had been made previously under the high rates, and there were so many of them on the street that those who didn't follow suit were starved out in short order; even the Yellow Cab Company had to come to it.

Due to the lack of a successful trade made, the Twentieth Century would have lost out if they hadn't organized their own insurance company, which has been very successful, has kept the insurance rates down for their own members and has forced the insurance companies to lower their rates.

I doubt if there is any business in which there is greater uncertainty and any more ruthless competition.

$7,000.00

There used to be an old fellow who played the McAlpin line. He was always talking about finding seven thousand dollars in the cab and retiring. The other drivers would say, "Well, did you find that seven thousand dollars yet?"

After every call he would search the cab. If he didn't the rest of us would, and at times pretend we had found it. We always had a lot of fun with him. He maintained that it could happen all right, big sums of money had been left in cabs, and if he got his hooks on that seven thousand, he would buy a little farm and retire from business.

One day after he had returned from a call and we were asking him if he had found the seven thousand dollars yet, the house detective came out and said, "Who took that last call?"

We told him. He asked where the cab was, and we pointed to the end of the line. The detective walked down there, reached in, and fetched out a wallet. He gave us the name of the man who had left it and said he had called up the hotel about it. After a few minutes the man who had lost the wallet arrived in another cab. He said, "There was seven thousand dollars in that wallet. He gave the detective one hundred dollars and the driver fifty dollars."

The poor old fellow stood there, looking down at the fifty in his hand, broken-hearted. He said, "I'll never get my seven thousand dollars now. A chance like that won't come twice."

THE LUSH

I stopped in at a Coffee Pot on Third Ave. and ran into Joe Lockwood. Joe says, "Jesus, I had a hot one the other night. I picked up a lush in Brooklyn for one of them swell apartment houses on Park Ave. about two o'clock in the morning. Well, when he gets there, he's passed out; couldn't wake him up. Well, I went through him. He didn't have much; none of them have any money. Beings I had two forty on the clock, I puts back in his pocket three bucks to pay the fare with. Then I goes in to see if I can get the door man to help get him out of the cab so as to have a witness and all that, and there was no door man on the job. Just then in comes a big swell-looking bird in a high hat, soup and fish, and I asks him if he knows the man in the cab, so he goes out, takes a look at him, and says, 'Why he lives here.' I says, 'Will you help me to get him out of the cab?' and he says, 'You'd better go to the corner and see if you can get a cop,' so I goes up to the corner. No cop. Then I looks back and I see the lush has come to and is climbing out the cab, and the swell bird is helping him. I walks back. They are talking together and the lush knows him all right. The lush says, 'Well, what do I owe you, driver?' and I says, Two-sixty.' He slicks his hands in his pants pockets, and don't get nothing; then he goes into his coat pockets, and don't get nothing; then he goes into his vest pockets, and I think, 'Now you got the right idea.' He turns his vest pockets out and the three bucks is gone. Well, I couldn't believe my own eyes. He says, 'If you will give me your name and address, I will send you a check to-morrow if that's all right with you.' I says, 'It's all right with me,' and I give him me name and address. And I did get a check, for a pound."

THE PARK

I had been working since early morning until about nine o'clock at night in the rain. Business had been good all day but I was about played out and was just going to turn in when another cab pulled up alongside of me with a flat. The driver says, "Do you want a good call?" Well, I thought I would take one more. Nothing like getting the money when you got the chance. So we opened the doors, and the couple climbed over into my cab.

The driver said, "Drive up to Central Park and drive around the Park. Go up some dark street."

I cut over to Ninth Ave. and up to 59th Street, into the Park and started around the Park.

I could hear them arguing back there and I thought to myself, "Keep it up old girl. The longer the argument, the more I make."

Well, I drove around the Park, and drove around again. They kept right on arguing, didn't say anything to me, so I kept on going around and around. It got mighty tiresome, with the rain drizzling down and the lights shining on the wet pavement. There was a knock in the motor that kept sounding louder and louder in the quiet of the Park. I tried going around the other way for a change. I drove around and around, around and around, and the motor kept sounding worse and worse and worse, and the lights flashed by shining on the pavement, harder and harder on my eyes. Then I tried doing figure eights, cutting across the middle of the Park. I did figure eights and figure eights. Then I started to do figure eights the other way. Still they kept on arguing. The knock in the motor got on my nerves until it felt like the whole machine was going to fall apart any minute. I got to thinking, "For God's sake quit arguing and let's get this over with."

Finally he gave it up, opened the front window and gave me an address downtown.

When we got down there, he said goodbye to the girl. She went in.

There was eighteen dollars and ten cents on the clock After going through all his pockets, all he could raise was seventeen sixty, so I took seventeen fifty and left him a dime for carfare.

JERRY

I was going up Fifth Ave. in the theatre rush and picked up a call for downtown. I saw a chance for a turn-around, so I stepped on it, but I didn't quite make it. Some bird cut me off and I got stuck half-way, and by the time I got straightened out, the cop had spotted me. He motioned me over to the curb. I pulled over. He started giving me a grand bawling out, and I figured I was sure in for a ticket, but I thought I would try talking to him, and I says, "Well, Jerry, it was this way."

"I ain't Jerry," he says. "Jerry was promoted."

"Why, that's right, you ain't him. You resemble him a lot, though. So Jerry is promoted. Well, he had it coming to him all right. He's a good scout."

So he says, "Well, go ahead now and watch your step."

EIGHTH AVENUE

I was cruising down Eighth Ave. late at night in the winter. A touring car in front of me ran over a man, so I pulled up at the curb like the rest of them to watch the show. There happened to be a cop right there, and they carried the fellow into the drug store on the corner. Quite a little crowd gathered outside. Then some gorilla in the crowd socked a guy and stretched him out cold in the street. Well, the crowd all drew back from him, and after he had lain there a minute or two I thought it was a darn shame to leave him lying there on a bitter cold night, so I says to another fellow, "Let's carry him in out of the weather." He takes him by the heels and I takes him by the shoulders, and we carried him into the drug store and we laid him down alongside the other fellow.

The cop looked up from his notes and says, "WHAT! Another one! Where'd he come from?"

The young fellow that was responsible for the accident rushed at me and grabbed me by the shoulders and says, "You think you're a wise guy, hunh? You're going to run another one in on me? Do you think you can get away with that stuff?"

And the Jewish proprietor of the store runs up and grabs me by the arm on the other side and says, "I'll have you understand this ain't no morgue, this is a business, and if you get any more, you take them somewhere else."

I thought I had better get out of there while I was all in one piece, so I backed out the door and on to the cab and decided to try Third Ave. for a while.

THE OLD COUPLE

While I was standing down at the City Hall, a man came along and said, "Take me over to the gin mill across from the Criminal Courts Building. You know the place." And I did.

He was a middle-aged man, quite prosperous and intelligent looking.

When we got over there he asked me to come in and have a drink, so I went in with him, on into the back room. There was a woman there who looked to be about sixty, very fat—soft pasty fat—thin and gray straggling hair. She had evidently been drinking a good deal. The man said, "This is my wife—my sweetheart."

We sat down with her and he ordered whiskey for three.

"We have been married thirteen years," he explained, "and we are having a little celebration."

She said, "He is the best husband in the world, only he makes too much money."

Just then the waiter came with the drinks. The man picked up his, held it up, and said, "Well, let's go."

As I drank mine, the woman said, "I don't like that 'Let's go.' That's a dirty word, that 'Let's go.'"

The man said, "She had me arrested yesterday. What do you think of that? But she didn't appear against me so the case was dismissed. Of course, if she had appeared against me, the Court would have looked at her, and I would have been dismissed."

She said, "When I came home last night the door was locked and I couldn't get in and he had some woman in there."

Bye and bye we went uptown, stopped at another gin mill in the Forties, and then we stopped at another one on East Twelfth Street. It was a macaroni factory, and we went back through all the machinery that wasn't working, and there was a gin mill in the rear. We had several drinks, and the man introduced us to the Italian proprietor. The woman put out her hand to shake hands with him, but he drew back and said, "I no maka da shake wid da lady. I maka da shake wid da man." They seemed quite put out, and the man explained that she was his wife. The proprietor said, "Oh yes, vera sweet girl."

The man bought a couple of quarts of whiskey at two fifty a quart, and they decided then to go home, so I drove than to their place down on the Bowery. The man went on up the stairs, and the woman tried to climb the stairs by pulling herself hand over hand up the banister, but she couldn't make it. Then I pushed her from behind and she hauled as hard as she could, so we finally got up the three flights of stairs, and the man had the door open.

They had one large three-cornered room with windows on two sides. It was crowded with old-fashioned furniture. There was an enormous black cat and a canary bird.

The woman sat down in the rocking chair, picked the cat up and said to me, "This is my baby."

The man poured out the whiskey for all three of us again. The woman started to cry. He said, "Don't cry, Mama," and he started the phonograph going, playing, "O Sol Mio." He put his hands up to his mouth and pretended to be producing the music on a mouth organ, rocked back and forth, and put all kinds of expression into it.

The woman rocked back and forth, petting the cat, and wept into her whiskey. When the song was finished, she said, "You must pay the chauffeur, John, because he's tooken such good care of us."

He jammed his hand down into his pocket, fetched out the roll, and handed it to me. There was about six dollars on the clock, so I peeled off seven and handed the rest back. Then I bid them good-bye and went back to work.

THE DEAD MAN

Early one morning I was passing the Polo Grounds on the 155th Street viaduct. My cap blew off and blew down into that lot alongside the Polo Grounds, so I drove on to where there is a stairway that leads down there, left the car, and walked down to get the hat.

Just at the bottom of that rocky cliff by the speedway there is a shallow pool of water. When I got down very close I saw there was a man lying in the water, so I went over to see what it was all about.

He was dead. An old man, a little old man with grey hair. He had put up a fight for it because his knuckles were all skinned up. He had a big, jagged gash in his forehead that went clear through, and his nose was broken.

I got to wondering how it had happened. He had evidently been carried there by people who thought the pool was deeper than it was because it was only deep enough to about half cover him. He must have been laid there by loving hands because he was laid out nice and straight with his hands folded over his breast, and his hat set up on a rock nearby. He was dressed in perfectly sound clothes—not old nor patched—but they were very cheap and unpressed. His shoes were old, had been soled, and had been polished at home.

He had one of those retreating chins, which is nevertheless very determined; his teeth turned in, the kind of mouth people have who are afraid to step out and fight in the open but who secretly by hook or by crook are determined to have their own way. He couldn't have been killed by professional criminals. They would have done a better job of it. He didn't look prosperous enough to attract robbers anyway. I imagine he was one of those little home tyrants whose slaves came to the end of their endurance at last, and then carried him out and left him with what respect they could.

GUN MEN

I was hanging out down at 4th Street and Sixth Avenue. Some very tough looking birds came over and wanted to know if I was looking for a job. I said, "Yes." They said they were watching a party who had copped one of their girls; if they came out and took a cab, they wanted to follow them, so I said I would hang around.

In a little bit the other party came out, grabbed a cab on the other side of the street. My party piled in and said, "Don't let them get away, and we'll make it right with you."

The other cab started up Sixth Avenue, with me after them. I followed them over to some third-rate hotel on the East Side. The cab stopped and I pulled up about one hundred yards behind them. My party all piled out and got behind my cab, peeking out, all with their hands to their hip pockets. The party in the lead spotted us then and they got in front of their cab with their hands at their hips. It left us drivers in a very unfortunate position.

Nothing happened.

The first party jumped back into their cab and started off again and me after them. They stepped on the gas and I stepped on the gas. Over to First Avenue, down to 17th, west on 17th to Third, up to 19th, west on 19th to Broadway, down to 15th, across 15th to Sixth, down Sixth to 4th, West Broadway to Houston, Houston to Greenwich, up Greenwich to 1st, over to the water front, down the water front to Desbrosses, going hell bent for election. They finally pulled up at another third-rate hotel on the West Side. My gang jumped out and got behind the car; the other gang jumped out and got in front of their car. Finally they all piled in and we started off again.

Over to Tenth, up Tenth wide open. Crossed over to the Park and started around the Park, taking the turns on two wheels. It was about two o'clock in the morning and we had it all to ourselves. We looped the loop around the Park a couple of times, then out, up Lenox and clear into the Bronx, up Southern Boulevard, crossed over to St. Ann's and up, back and forth around the Bronx. Finally, back down Willis and First Avenue to Greenwich Village. Stopped at another third-class hotel. Both parties jumped out again, then piled in. We started off once more.

We finally wound up at a Black and Tan cabaret on 137th Street near Seventh. The first party paid their cab driver off and went into the cabaret, so my outfit paid me off.

I rolled up alongside the first cab and said, "Well, we had a nice ride, huh?"

"Yeh," he said. "What do you say we go have a cup of coffee?"

We pulled up to a one-arm lunch, went in and got a cup of coffee.

He said, "By God, I was afraid I had lost you there a couple of times."

THE ADDICT

I picked up a couple one night and when I got them to their destination, they handed me the money but hesitated about getting out. They were rather poor-looking people, about thirty, apparently husband and wife. Then the man stammered a bit and asked me if I knew where a person could go to take the drug cure. I told him I didn't know but I understood the city ran a kind of place where they put people through a cure. He went on to explain he had got started taking drugs and the woman chipped in and helped along. I finally got it clear that he had become addicted to drugs through taking stuff for insomnia and now was in a pretty bad way, and it took so much to keep him going, he couldn't make both ends meet any more, and he wanted to get over it some way. I suggested the best thing to do would be to call up the Board of Health and they ought to give him the information. They wanted to know if they could hire me the next morning if I would attend to it for them, so I said I would.

I called and got the man the next morning. His wife had gone to work apparently. The man looked to be in very bad shape. He said he had been off the stuff for a day and wasn't going to buy any more. I called up the Board of Health. Some girl answered the phone and I told her I wanted to find out about getting a man sent to the City institution for drug addicts. She said, "You will have to come down and see the Health Commission."

I drove down to the Health Department building near City Hall, left the man in the car, went up to the office and told the girl at the desk my business. She told me to sit down and wait; she would tell the Commissioner. I sat down and waited and waited. After about an hour the Commissioner came out. A woman who had come in in the meantime rushed up and started talking to him. I thought, "Well, I will wait until she gets through instead of raising a disturbance." Bye and bye she got through and the Commissioner turned and started to go back into his office. I jumped up and said, "Hey, do you realize I have been waiting over an hour to talk to you?"

"Well, why don't you say what you want?"

So I told him the story.

"Why, we have nothing to do with that business," he explained. "You will have to go see the Board of Narcotic Control."

"Where can I find them?" I asked.

"The girl will look up their address for you."

So the girl went through some papers in her desk and told me to go to 148 Bowery, I think. I drove over to the Bowery, went up to a dingy office with a lot of benches around for people to sit on, and a shabby old man at the desk. I told him the story.

He said, "You will have to wait until Mrs. ————— comes in. She attends to that. Sit down. She will be in pretty soon."

I was getting worried about the poor devil in the cab. He looked pretty bad. I was afraid he might pass out on me, so I went down, helped him up the steps, and put him on a bench, so I could have him where I could watch him.

We waited and we waited and waited.

Finally I went up to the desk again and said, "What's the idea? When is this woman going to get in anyway?"

"Well, I can't make her come in. You will have to be patient. You should realize you are getting all of this service for nothing and appreciate it."

"Yes, and it seems to be worth it."

I sat down and we waited. Finally the woman came in and after fussing around at her desk for fifteen or twenty minutes, she asked me what I wanted and I told her the story.

She got out a blank and said, "Now, what's your name?"

I told her.

"How long have you been addicted?"

I explained courteously I wasn't addicted.

She continued, "How many members of your family are addicted?"

"My family hasn't got anything to do with it. This fellow wants to take the cure and I want to get him through it."

She said, "Well, you will have to give me all the facts if we are going to do anything for you. We want to do all we can for you but we must know the facts."

I said, "If you want to take down this man's name and have him committed, all right. If you don't, say so."

She grumbled a little bit and wrote the man's name and address down. Then she wanted to know how many members of his family were addicted. I told her I didn't know and I didn't care. Then she went on to explain about how whole families get to taking the stuff, it's so terrible, and so on and so on, what a time they have helping them.

Finally I asked, "Well, what do you do next?"

She looked at her watch and looked at the calendar and said, "It's too late for us to do anything to-day, but maybe if you go up to the other office on 125th Street they will be able to take care of you. You had better go up to see them. I don't think I will be able to do anything for you." She gave me the address on 125th Street.

I lugged the poor devil back to the cab, and we rolled up to 125th Street. I left him in the cab and went upstairs, told the woman in charge there I had a man I wanted to have committed as a drug addict.

She got out a blank and put down my name and address. I told her I didn't enter into it; the other fellow wanted to be committed. But she insisted on taking it down.

"How long have you been addicted?" she asked.

I told her I wasn't addicted. I had a fellow out in the cab I wanted to get committed.

Finally she put down his name and address. Then she said, "How many other members of your family are addicted to the use of narcotics?"

I explained over again I wasn't addicted, my family had nothing to do with it, and I knew nothing about the other fellow's family.

She said, "Now, are you sure you are not taking it yourself?"

I said, "Well, for God's sake, let's get some action. That poor devil's likely to pass out on me down there."

"Well, we can't do anything about it today."

"Can't you send him to a hospital or something?" I asked.

"No," she explained. "The hospitals won't accept anything but ambulance cases, and he isn't an ambulance case as long as he is in a taxicab. No," she continued, "all you can do is to take him down to the other office on the Bowery at nine o'clock Thursday morning. That's the office for receiving."

"Well," I said, "from the way it looks to me this guy will be dead before that time."

"Then you had better get him some of the stuff to tide him over until Thursday morning."

"Where can I get some of it?"

She opened her mouth to answer, then changed her mind. Finally she said, "Well, you ought to be able to get some of it. There are plenty of places."

I went down to see how the passenger was getting along, and he was about gone. He had been throwing up green stuff and had straightened out as stiff as a board in the cab. I couldn't bend his arms or his legs. His face had turned a kind of a yellowish green. I managed to get out of him where we could get some of the stuff, so I drove over there, got a small bottle of it for five bucks. He took a small shot and commenced to feel better right away, so I took him home and arranged to call for him Thursday morning.

When I got over there for him Thursday morning he was in pretty good shape. The supply had lasted him. I took him down to the Bowery. We waited from nine until about quarter past ten, and the woman hadn't showed up yet. Finally she came in in a great rush and said, "Oh, you are here. Well, now, let's see. I have a great deal to attend to today. I don't believe I will be able to go over with you, but you can go over there yourself. It's 301 Mott Street, and they will tell you where you go there."

I felt right at home, then, because 301 Mott Street is the Traffic Court, where I have been so often and spent so much good jack.

I drove right over there and asked one of the cops where you go to get a drug addict committed. He gave me the number of the room, and, by jinks, it was the same old room where I had been three or four times previously, where I with a number of others had pleaded guilty and were fined in a bunch.

We went into the room and I said to the clerk, "I have been sent here by the Board of Narcotic Control. I have a man here to take the drug cure. The Board of Narcotic Control told me—"

"We don't care anything about that," he interrupted. "All you got to do is give his name. Anybody can come in here and be committed to take the cure that wants to."

That's all there was to it. The man signed his name. The clerk took it into the Judge and he signed it. And we were through.

THE TRUE JOY OF LIVING

He wanted me to stay with him for a while and having gone that far with it I thought I might as well see it through. We waited in the room with the court clerk while the rest of the addicts were being signed up. About a dozen accumulated there. One man objected to the terms of the paper they all had to sign. He said he wasn't going to accept such conditions; he was no common criminal. The clerk said, "Don't sign it then. I don't give a damn if you sign it or not."

There was an in-drawing of breaths among the addicts and indignant murmurs. One said, "He's got no heart. He wouldn't care if a man died."

The clerk said, "Of course not. An addict is no good to himself or anybody else. An addict is yellow. The sooner you're dead the better. You can walk out of here any time you want to. No one is holding you."

They all subsided and looked kind of disappointed. The man signed the paper. Presently a cop came along and told us to follow him. He led us down to a barred room in the cellar. The addicts were all indignation again. They said, "They treat you like a dog."

"Common criminals."

"See, the windows are barred."

The cop said, "Till the wagon comes you got to stay here. You can beat it then if you want to. There'll be no one to guard you and the back of the wagon is open."

They all looked disappointed again. A big wop said to me, "Is this your first cure?"

My addict said, "He ain't taking the cure; he's just riding out with me."

"I took the cure ten or twelve times," said the wop. "This cure is no good. The best cure I ever took was the Riverside. That was when Copeland was commissioner. Ah, he was a fine man. He was the friend of the hop-heads. We had fine rooms and books and pianos. They couldn't keep it up. These guys don't appreciate them things. They tore up the books and ripped the pianos apart. They had to close it down, but it was a fine cure; Dr. Copeland is a fine man. I ought to know; I took all the cures."

They had all taken the cure several times. It seemed that they keep needing more and more till they can't make enough to buy it and so they take the cure so as to be able to start over again. It was agreed that sooner or later you take to using the needle; you get the best kick out of it that way. The big wop got out his outfit and said he might as well have a shot. He had the outfit wrapped up in a handkerchief, a bottle of the stuff, a hypodermic, a spoon with the handle cut off and a candle with which to heat the solution in the spoon. They all had a shot and several offered me some. They said I might as well use it as it would all be taken away from them when they got to the island.

Then the cop came and unlocked the door and we all went out and climbed into the wagon, a bus, and started for Blackwell's Island. It seemed to me that the addicts eyed the open rear door of the bus rather resentfully.

There was a little fellow there named Thompson. He got to talking to my man. He said he did house work, beating rugs and cleaning and so on for a living. He said he was getting along all right but he got a bottle of the stuff that was no good. It was just milk sugar or something. He didn't have any more money and he nearly went crazy that night and he had a terrible time working the next day to get money to buy some more. Then none of the people he knew had any of the stuff and he want chasing all over Brooklyn trying to find some. He finally got a bottle but it was so diluted so it was hardly any good so he decided to take the cure.

He was a Christian, and my man, who was an atheist, got into a hot argument with him over religion. Thompson said he believed in God and Jesus and expected to go to heaven.

My man said, "You must get all that stuff out of your head. Read Nietzsche, read Schopenhauer, read his 'Studies in Pessimism.' Until you get this Christ stuff out of your head you'll never be able to appreciate the true joy of living."

I got off at the Island and went back and went to work.

NOT WHAT I USED TO BE

Driving a taxi is pretty wearing on a man; looking and looking all the time all set to jump for a call. There is no exercise about it to keep you in trim. After about seven years of hacking I commenced to find that I wasn't what I used to be. I picked up a man at a hospital who was taking his wife home after an operation. When I got them to their place in the Bronx the woman discovered that she wasn't as well as she thought she was. She couldn't get out of the cab. The man was elderly and he didn't know what he was going to do. He said they lived four flights up. Without stopping to think I said, "Why, I'll carry her up."

When I lifted her out of the cab. I commenced to wonder if I had made a mistake. She weighed about a hundred and fifty pounds and by the time I had climbed two flights of stairs I was so far gone I nearly dropped her. I had to back up against the wall and rest her on one knee while I got my breath before I could make the last two flights.

THE FORD AND CHATHAM SQUARE

I bought a Ford taxi painted brown and white and made much better money for a time cruising for business at the then low rate of thirty cents a mile than I had made before bucking the lines, but as time went on more and more cabs were painted brown and white, a lot of the cab stands were abandoned, and there got to be more cabs cruising than there was business, so I tried playing some of the old deserted stands again.

I picked out one on Seventh Avenue and did pretty well there, but the others who saw me standing there took to playing the stand too, so pretty soon there were eight or ten cabs on the stand. Then some of the old-time buckers came back on the stand with high-rate clocks. They claimed that the stand was an old buckers' stand and it rightly belonged to them. One by one they managed to chase the low-rate men off the stand, and finally I was the only one left. As long as I played the stand, I naturally got the preference with a low-rate clock, and the buckers, of course, didn't like that, so I finally decided I couldn't hold the thing down all by myself.

I went to another one of the old-time abandoned stands. The same thing happened there.

Finally I tried standing at Chatham Square at the corner of Mott Street, which is Chinatown. I did well there for quite a while as the drivers of low-rate cabs weren't so quick to line up behind me on the stand because the neighborhood has a very bad reputation.

I found the Chinese to be very good customers. I didn't overcharge them, and they appreciated the fact and gave me lots of good business.

It was quite an interesting location. There is supposed to be a cop on post there all the time, and the cops and plain clothes men were passing all the time. In spite of this fact, a couple of pickpockets used to hang out on the corner there in front of the cigar store. I got quite well acquainted with them. They didn't seem to be at all reticent about the business. The little thin one who did the real work showed up in a nice new suit one day and I spoke about it. He said, "Yes, I have been needing a suit for a long time, but business has been terrible. You have no idea. I ordered this suit made quite a while ago, paid a deposit on it, but couldn't get it out. I promised the tailor to get it out yesterday. I got up in the morning and I just had carfare. Well, coming down on the car I got a guy for sixteen dollars. The conny (conductor) was one of these fifty-fifty guys. I told him I only got six and gave him three. I should give him eight. What did he do to earn it? That give me thirteen, and I owed thirty-five on the suit. Well, I changed to another car and got another guy for ten. By the time I got down here I had enough to get the suit out, and now I'm broke again."

I says, "How is it about getting caught? Have much trouble that way?"

"Oh," he says, "It's bad now. It ain't what it used to be. It used to be that if you got a stretch the Warden would let you out if he knew you, and all you had to do was to show up when he needed you, when the inspectors were around or something like that and turn him in a bit every day. But that's no good any more. A lot of crooks got into the game and didn't show up when he told them to and got him into a jam. You can't blame him; he's got to protect himself."

FRISKING

I was standing at Chatham Square one Saturday afternoon and picked up a young man who had evidently just got his week's pay and was starting out on a gay time. He had me drive him over to Brooklyn, stopped at a gin mill. Bye and bye he came out and had me drive him to another gin mill. After about six of these stops, he appeared to be in a bad way and told me to drive back to Chatham Square. Before he got there he changed the address; before I got to that address, he had changed it again, and then he fell asleep. I tried to wake him but didn't get anything out of him. I didn't know where he lived or what to do with him. I commenced to wonder if he had any money left to pay the fare with, so I pulled up at a quiet spot and went through him. He had about forty dollars on him. I said to myself, "He's going to lose this sure; I might as well have it as somebody else," so I put ten back, figuring that would pay the fare and leave a little something. It was a wonder to me he had anything left by that time.

I thought probably he lived somewhere in the neighborhood of Chatham Square, so I decided to go back there and then wake him up to see if I could get his address out of him. I drove back to the same old corner, tried to wake him up, but couldn't get a thing out of him. Then I walked up to the corner to see if I could get a cop to take him in charge. Just as I got to the corner I saw one of my pickpocket friends walking toward the cab. I thought of the ten and hustled back. He just opened the cab door and closed it again, so I knew everything was all right, but I stood close by the cab and waited for a cop to come along. Finally one showed up and I told him about the fellow, that I couldn't wake him up, and we drove over to the police station.

The sergeant told the cops to take him into the back room and wake him up and then bring him out and search him. It seems there is a rule that a prisoner is not supposed to be searched except in front of the sergeant's desk.

They threw water on him, twisted his ears, slapped his face, and banged him around. Still he didn't come to, so they started searching him. The cop found about fifty cents in change in his watch pocket. The ten was gone.

When the cop found the fifty cents, the colored porter looked at the cop. The cop looked at the porter. The porter looked at me.

The cop looked at me. The porter said, "Put it back; put it back. You won't get it. Somebody will get it, but you won't get it."

They put everything back in his pockets and started trying to bring him to, throwing water, twisting his ears, slapping him around, and finally he came to.

They stood him up in front of the sergeant then and he cried and sobbed and said he had been misused. They searched him over again and put everything he had on the desk.

The sergeant asked me how much I had on the clock. I had about four dollars. He asked the man if he had any relatives who would be able to pay the fare if I took him home, and the man said, "No."

"Well." said the sergeant, "do you want me to lock this man up?"

I said, "Why, no. If he hasn't got the money, he hasn't got it. It will be no consolation to me to have him held in jail."

"Well," said the sergeant, "you can have this fifty cents anyway."

"Oh," I said, "he needs some carfare. If I'm going to lose it, I might as well lose it. Fifty cents won't do me any particular good."

The sergeant then gave him a long lecture on what a decent fellow I was and how he should appreciate all I was doing for him.

I offered to ride him in the cab over to the subway, but his appetite for riding in taxis was gone. He turned down the offer.

THE POWER OF MONEY

I was driving down William Street one day and a man started walking across in front of me, and I put on the brake. Then he started to run, and as there was plenty of room, I let the brake off. Then he stopped running before he got out of the way, and I had to slap the brake on short and cut to one side to keep from hitting him. Then he made a last frightened jump for it after I was already clear of him. I drove on and thought no more of it, but I got held up in traffic down the block a ways, and the first thing you know this man comes along with a cop and tells the cop, "Here's that smart taxi driver who nearly ran over me."

The cop seemed reluctant to join in. He said to me, "Well, what about it?"

I said, "Why this bird goes skipping across William Street, then stops short in front of me. My idea is if he would look where he's going, he would keep out of trouble."

The man said, "I will teach you a lesson," and to the cop, "I want this man arrested."

The cop said, "I can't arrest him. I didn't see it and have no authority for making the arrest. But if you want to arrest him, all right, go ahead."

The man insisted that the cop arrest me. Finally the cop said, "If you want to drive over to the station house, let's drive over and get this over."

I said, "I'll take you over but he can either walk or get another cab. I'll be damned if he is going to get in my cab."

He got another cab. We drove over to the same station house where I had taken the drunk in the previous story.

The man said to the desk-sergeant, "I want this man locked up for reckless driving. He came through William Street at about thirty miles an hour and would have run over me if I hadn't been quick enough to jump out of the way."

While he was talking, the cop pulled me off to one side and said, "This bird is a big man in Wall Street and he can make a lot of trouble for you, and for us too. Now I would advise you to go easy and get out of it."

I said, "To hell with him. I wish I had run over him."

"Well," the cop advised, "go as easy as you can."

The sergeant called me over and wanted to know what I had to say.

"Why," I said, "this bird comes skipping across the street like a fairy. I slowed down for him, then he started running so I let the brake off; then he stopped again right in front of me. Let him make all the charges he wants. He didn't get hit. I wasn't going fast. My word's as good as his, or better."

The sergeant got down behind the desk and took me over to one side and said, "Now, this man has got a lot of influence in the financial district. He's a big man and can make a lot of trouble for you and for me too, and I would advise you to go slow. Now, if you will say you are sorry that will give me an excuse for refusing to go through with it."

"Sorry hell. The only thing I'm sorry for is that I didn't get the —————— —————— —————— ——————."

"Now, now. Keep your temper. Don't fly off the handle like that," the sergeant said and climbed back on his seat behind the desk, turned to the man and said, "Now, I think this young man realizes that he has made a mistake and will be more careful in the future. I am going to make a report of this case to turn in and if anything of the sort happens in the future, it will go hard with him."

The man said, "If it weren't for my respect for the law I would teach him a lesson with my own hands."

I turned on him. "Well, you can have an opportunity any time you want it."

The sergeant said, "There, there now. That's enough of that," as he handed me my book and badge and motioned me out.

$5,000 IN CHINKS

While I was standing at Chatham Square a white man came along and said he needed four cabs and would I get three more for him and drive to No. 8 Pell Street. I got three more cabs and led the procession around to Pell Street. The man brought out a crowd of Chinamen and loaded them up, five in each cab. Then he told me that he wanted to take them all up to Grand Central. He said these men were sailors on a British ship and in order to be allowed ashore the ship owners had to put up a thousand dollars with the Government for each man to guarantee their return to the ship. He was taking them up to Boston to go out on another ship belonging to the same company.

When I got to Grand Central one of the cabs with his five thousand dollars' worth of Chinamen wasn't there. We waited and watched and the white man got more and more excited. Finally it showed up and the driver said we drove too fast for him.

THE MISSIONARY

The United States Army recruiting office used to keep a sergeant stationed at Chatham Square with an advertising sign to get recruits. White I was standing there I got to talking to him. A missionary for one of the Bowery missions came along handing out tracts. He gave each of us one.

I looked at the sergeant and said, "I'm afraid you can't do much business here; you picked out a couple of pretty hard customers."

The missionary was a big, thick set, red-faced Scandinavian. He looked at us and, abandoning the sanctified air for a moment, said, "Well, I'll tell you. I used to be a carpenter and I worked hard all the time. I used to come down here on the Bowery on pay day, spend all my money in gin mills. I never had anything. And then I got religion at the Bowery Mission." As he continued his voice gradually increased in volume to the true camp meeting boom, "Now I got three houses; Praise the Lord. I got three square meals in a day; BLESS HIS DEAR NAME. I got plenty of money and nothing to worry about; GLORY BE TO GOD." He smiled very triumphantly as he walked off.

The sergeant said, "By God, you know, he's got the right idea after all."

THROGGS NECK

I got home late for supper and told my wife that I had had a call to Throggs Neck and didn't want to turn it down.

She said, "Where?"

"Throggs Neck."

"Where?"

"Throggs Neck."

"I can't tell what you're talking about," she said. "It sounds just like 'Throggs Neck!'"

CANADA BY NINE IN THE MORNING

I stopped in at a restaurant late one night and Charlie Mack came in. He is one of the old timers that I met when I was playing the buckers' lines. He looked very prosperous. I remarked on it.

He says, "Yeh, I fell into it. I'd just pulled into the garage for the night when a guy comes in and says he wants a cab to go to Canada. He wants to get there by nine o'clock the next morning. He says he'll pay well for it. Just joking I said I would get him there by nine o'clock for five hundred dollars. He pulled out a roll of yellow bills that would choke a horse, on the level, it would choke a horse, and peeled off five hundred. I got kind of leery then because I couldn't make Canada by nine o'clock in the morning, so I says I would have to have somebody go along with me. Jack was just pulling in and he said he would come along. The guy give him fifty."

"Well." I said, "what did you do?"

"Oh," he said, "when we got up to Ossining he wanted to get out for a minute, and as soon as he is out I stepped on the gas and we came on back again. Huh, Canada by nine o'clock in the morning."

GOT IT LEGITIMATE

I got to talking to another hack driver in a restaurant the other night. He said he wasn't doing very well, had kind of lost his nerve, he'd run over a woman and killed her last week. "I didn't feel upset at the time," he said, "but it's kind of got me now. She didn't die right away. I put her in the cab and took her over to the hospital and went from there to the station house to make the report. I wasn't feeling upset. I walked in, threw my coat open, handed him my badge, and book, and stuff. But you know I carried a rod under my left arm and when I threw my coat open, the cops, of course, saw the thing; they thought they had me, but I got a license to carry it. I flashed that and it was all right. I got the license legitimate," he explained. "I used to drive a truck, running booze for a bootlegger and the boss got it for me."

"Well, what happened to the woman?" I asked.

"Why," he said, "they discharged her from the hospital the next day and the day after that she died. The police were going to break my license for it, but my old boss squared that."

SOLD THE FORD

I finally decided that I had better sell my Ford taxi and buy a new one, but I thought it a good idea to work for other people and try out the various makes of cars at somebody else's expense before I made a decision as to what to get.

Harry Day, the owner of the Day Taxi Corporation had recently bought five hundred Yellow cabs and had obtained the concession at Grand Central and Penn Station. I went over to their garage on 49th Street and applied for a job. I was sent out with another applicant and a mechanic for a tryout. While I had driven plenty of gearshift cars years before, I had been driving that one Ford for so long that I had gotten so it was a part of me, like my own hands and feet. I didn't have to think about anything any more. I just thought "stop" and I stopped; I thought "start" and I started. When I took the wheel on the Yellow cab, I was all at sea. I shoved the clutch in expecting the car to go ahead in low. Nothing happened. Then I had to think about shifting gears. When I wanted to give it more gas, I would start scratching around under the steering wheel for the throttle, and there wasn't any. Then it would occur to me I had to step on it. So I didn't make a very good showing. The other fellow, however, made out all right as he had been driving a Shaw previously.

We all went back to the employment office and the mechanic told the employment office man something in private and went out. Then the employment manager took down my name and address, license numbers, etc., and gave me a badge, and I was all set to go to work, and he told me to report at the 25th Street garage. Then he turned to the other fellow and said, "I am afraid you haven't had enough experience; you had better go to work for somebody else for a while and then come back."

I saw the employment manager had got us mixed. When the other fellow started in to explain that he had been driving a Yellow right along and knew all about them, the employment manager caught on he had made a mistake, but he didn't want to admit it, so I backed on out the door. I knew the other fellow could come back the next day and get a job if he wanted to and I also knew that with a few hours' practice I would be perfectly familiar with the Yellow.

WORKING FOR DAY

I reported at the 25th Street garage that evening ready to go to work on the night line. It was an interesting bunch of men waiting for the cars to come in.

Harry Day had been brought up in Hell's Kitchen and had been a taxi driver, playing closed lines on the water front. When prohibition came along, he got into the bootlegging game and made rapid strides. Possibly his success was due to the fact that he already knew the best of the gunmen and gorillas in New York that were necessary to the business. When he was at the high tide of his success, he bought five hundred Yellow cabs at a crack, got concessions at Grand Central and Penn Station and put all the gorillas in Hell's Kitchen to work driving them. When a West Side gunman got out of Sing Sing, Harry was there to meet him and gave him a job. Most of the drivers were gorillas. The mechanics were gorillas. The checkers were gorillas. The garage superintendent was an ex-heavyweight prize fighter of considerable ability. Even the bookkeepers in his office on Times Square were gorillas.

I went very carefully about breaking in on the job. Whenever anyone spoke it had the effect of a threat. One of the drivers asked the superintendent if his car hadn't come in yet and the superintendent said, "How long have you been working around here? Did you ever get a poke in the nose?" I gave my name and waited quietly until my name was called. I got on the car and got out of the garage very carefully.

I made out very well that night and pulled in about two o'clock in the morning and discovered that we were expected to line up the cars in a certain way outside to drive into the garage. A man at the door would holler out, "All right there" when there was room for another cab to come in.

When you got inside you took gasoline. Then some one said, "Pull up" as though it would be your last moment if you didn't. You then pulled up to the wash stand and somebody said, "Stop." Then a man came around with a box with coins in it which he shook and said, "Put something in the kitty, coffee money for the boys." Nobody dared refuse.

The second night I took a chance and said, "I don't think you boys ought to drink so much coffee; it's bad for you," and didn't put anything in the kitty. Nothing happened, I think, probably because they were so surprised they didn't know what to make of it.

That same night I reported that the rear end didn't sound quite right, for having driven my own cab I knew it was better to take care of those things first rather than last. I made the report to the head mechanic. He said, "What? What did you say?" I thought my last moment had come. But I stuck to it, so he jacked the rear end up and gave it a tryout, and great was my relief when he did hear something wrong in it.

One night the superintendent knocked five drivers cold, one right after another, for not pulling up and stopping their cars just to suit him.

There were certain great advantages in working for Day. For one thing he squashed all summonses. If you got a summons for anything, you turned it into the office and paid no more attention to it. He had to cut that out after a while for his own protection because the drivers got to going so wild they smashed up all the cars. Along about two o'clock in the morning they used to come west on 49th Street and on 25th Street to the two garages in a more or less steady stream and crossed Ninth and Tenth Avenues so recklessly that it became customary for the street car motorman on those Avenues to stop at 49th Street and 25th Street while the conductor went ahead to see if the coast was clear.

Now there were lots of closed lines at that time, a closed line being a hack stand held down by a bunch of good fighters who beat up any driver who dares to get a call in that immediate neighborhood. But Harry kept a big Packard car, loaded full of gorillas, standing by the Pennsylvania Hotel, and if a Day driver got beat up for chiseling a call on any one of those closed lines, he could telephone the office. I was down at South Ferry once when one of Day's drivers got beat up. In a little while the big Packard appeared. Its occupants came down and each one hired a cab. Then they all drove up somewhere on Greenwich Street. The passengers got out and from then on you couldn't hear anything but crack, bang, sock. There wasn't anybody able to work the South Ferry line for several days.

After a few of these events word got passed around and Day drivers went unmolested although the buckers who used to work the West Shore Ferry line dared to try cutting tires on Day cabs when they worked there. Day's gorillas came down one night and cleaned them up so thoroughly that their cars were left standing there all the next day. Even their friends were afraid to come down and drive their cars away.

There had been a particularly tough bunch in a line on West 4th Street. One of Day's drivers picked up a call near there one night, and one of the members of the line threatened him. The Day man stepped down off his cab and the other fellow hit him. The Day man knocked the bucker down and just then a cop came up and was going to put the Day driver under arrest for assault. The rest of the line rushed up then and told the cop that it was only their own man's fault, that he started it; and they gave their own member warning that if he ever slugged any Day drivers around there, he could get the hell off the line.

THE BENEVOLENT AUTOCRAT

I went up to the office the next week to get my pay. Another driver there said, "Say, Harry, I want to borrow fifteen dollars."

Harry said, "What do you want with fifteen dollars?"

"I want to get a dress for the wife."

Harry said, "Go on. How can you get a dress for the wife with fifteen dollars?" and pushed him in the face.

The driver said, "Well, I got twenty-five and with fifteen more I can get her a decent dress."

Harry called out to the cashier, "Give him fifteen dollars."

I found that Harry took care of the families of many of the men who were taken sick, sent their sick children to the country, paid their doctor bills. On the other hand, if a driver was caught riding stick up (carrying a passenger with the flag up so the meter wouldn't register so as to keep the fare) the gorillas would pick him up at night and give him the finest shellacking you ever saw.

In spite of all Day's generosity and all the beatings that were handed out, the drivers kept right on riding stick up. I think they cheated Day more than any other cab owner in town.

One driver had been sick a couple of months and his family had been sick. Day had supported them, sent them all to the country, kept the family there a long time. And after all that they got him riding stick up one night. When the gorillas got through with him, he was a sight to behold.

I rode stick up on him myself, made a flat rate to the Bronx one night. I got up to 125th Street when I spotted Harry and the gorillas in the big Packard. I put the flag down real quick and they pulled up alongside of me. He says, "Got a good call?"

I said, "Yeh, Bronx."

One of the gorillas got out and looked over the seals on the clock, but he didn't look to see what the clock registered. If he had seen there was only twenty cents on it, my goose would have been cooked.

When Day had been running the cabs a year he gave a dinner, for all drivers who had been with him over ten months, at the Pennsylvania Hotel, gave them all gold badges, took them up to the Follies in taxicabs. Under the excitement of the occasion the gorillas socked all the buckers playing the big Pennsylvania Hotel line and put Day cabs on the line in their place.

One of the drivers was held up one night by five men, who got about thirty-five dollars off of him and took the cab. He went up to the office and told Harry about it, described the men. Harry made good the money he had lost and told him not to say anything to the police about it.

In the meantime the five men had had an accident with the car and the police had picked them up, found the driver had no hack license, and knew the car was stolen. The police tried to get Day and the driver to appear against them, but Day refused so the police had to turn them loose, which might seem very generous, but the gorillas picked them up about as soon as they got out and beat hell out of them.

THE MASTER OF HELL'S KITCHEN

I picked up four young toughs on Ninth Avenue one night. I would have passed them up if I hadn't been working for Day, because from the looks of them it was to be expected that they would hold me up or refuse to pay the fare or beat me up for the fun of it or something of the sort. They were apparently making arrangements for a dance, and we made a number of stops in Hell's Kitchen while they talked to people, principally at gin mills. Then we rolled over to the East Side, all around there, stopping at gin mills while they talked to other rough necks. Finally they had me drive them to 38th Street between Tenth and Eleventh Avenues. They said they would be right back. They hadn't said that before so I took that to mean they would run out on me, but there wasn't anything I could do about it. They went into one of the tenements and after a minute or two I followed them. One of them was pretty drunk and could hardly walk. I heard the other three in the dark talking about what they would do with him. One said, "We can get away all right, but what are we going to do with him? He's helpless."

I went back to the cab and drove up to the office on Broadway at 45th Street. Jimmy O'Donnell was in the office with a couple of others. He is an old-time gunman grown somewhat conservative. I told him all about it, what they looked like and where I had taken them. He said to the other men, "Well, we will go get that dough in the morning. The last time I went over there to collect a lousy three dollars, there was lead, yeh, soft lead. We'll go in the morning."

Just then Tommy O'Neil came in. He is, I guess, about the most feared one in the whole outfit, a small slender, quiet young fellow, rather unhealthy looking. If it weren't for his eyes, you would never suspect there is anything extraordinary about him at all. He asked me what it was and I told him some guys gave me a ride, what they looked like and where I took them.

He says, "I know who they are. I'll get it. You go ahead and hack and by the time you turn in I'll have the dough at the garage for you."

When I turned in that night the cashier said, "Here's something O'Neil left for you." It was an envelope containing the amount of the fare plus a very handsome tip.

RICH UNCLE

While I was driving for Harry Day I picked up a young fellow downtown late one night who said to drive to 38th Street and Tenth Avenue. On the way he sat on one of the front seats so he could talk to me.

He said, "I'm going to see my uncle. I never knew I had an uncle till last week. I thought all my folks were dead. I was born and raised over there in Hell's Kitchen. I'm married now; got three kids. We live way out in Brooklyn. My uncle doesn't look like much but he's there. He's strong. Anybody can find it out that goes against him. He's a Federal prohibition agent. That's why I picked a Day cab. He's in with Day. He said, 'Never hire anything but a Day taxi.' Oh, he's well fixed. He owns houses over there. Buys another one every week or so. I'm glad I found him. It ain't so good being alone with no relatives."

We reached 38th Street and Tenth Avenue and drove east until we came to the No Name Club, where he had me stop. In that region at all hours of the night there are always a number of young men standing around in doorways. They seldom speak to each other and then very low. They always stand with their backs to something, on the balls of their feet, their eyes alert, and their hands near their belts. Some of them came over to look us over. The young fellow told them he was looking for John Ford. They said he had been to the club that night but thought he had gone to the Milk Dairy, so we drove around into 37th Street to a dairy. And there some of the young toughs stepped over to look us over. At the mention of Ford's name they too seemed to accept us as all right. They said we might wait for him, that he was likely to come around. They retired to their places.

We waited and the young man continued his talk about his uncle and himself. He said he was working as an electrician and made good pay, that a family was a big obligation, that it was nice to have relatives. He seemed thin and overworked and pathetic, not at all like the rest of Hell's Kitchen.

Two cops came along walking in the middle of the street. He said, "That's no good. They can get them easy off the roofs."

After a while one of the toughs suggested another place we might find Ford. After much driving around and waiting we found him at a gin mill on Ninth Avenue. He was a plump little sharp-eyed man. He received his nephew very cordially, but it seemed a little forced. He told me what a fine man Day was and that he did lots of business with him. He set up whiskey for us, which the proprietor refused to take pay for. He got out his gold badge and showed us his credentials as a Federal prohibition agent. The young fellow ran on about how glad he was to see him.

They got into the cab and we visited several other gin mills, where the uncle was received with marked respect and introduced us to the owners. We had more whiskey, and they fell into an argument as to which are the best, the Jews or the Irish.

"The Jews are the best people in the world," the uncle said, "the Turkeys are no good."

The nephew said, "Where do you get that stuff? Ain't we both Irish?"

The uncle said, "Never mind. The Turkeys are no good."

And on and on.

At last the uncle said, "Well, I tell ye now, I'm right. A Jew will come across but a Turkey will go to the station house."

The uncle at last persuaded the young fellow that it was time to go home. He got me off to one side, and I hoped he was going to pay the fare for the boy, but he said, "Treat him right. Don't overcharge him too much; he's just a workin' feller." So I took the nephew over to the subway and really felt sorry there was so much on the clock.

A WESTERN UNION MESSENGER

I was going through Hell's Kitchen one night and saw a Western Union messenger delivering a message. Later on when I was standing over on Fifth Avenue the same messenger came along. I said, "How do you like delivering messages over in that district?"

He stopped, smiled, and said, "Oh all right. I'll never forget the first one I took over there. I had a telegram for some fellow named Conners on 38th Street west of Ninth Avenue. I found the number. It was a tenement house, but there weren't any names on the bells in the vestibule, so I went inside and looked for names on the doors. There weren't any names on the doors on the first floor so I went up to the second floor, and there weren't any names there, so I thought I would knock on a door and ask if anybody knew where this guy lived. I knocked on one. The door opened just a crack and I saw a man with a big club. He looked at me and said, 'Oh, it's Western Union.' I asked him if Conners lived there. He thought a minute and said, 'No.' I said. 'Do you know where he does live?' 'No, I don't know of anybody by that name in this house.' I said, 'Well, I'll try upstairs.' He said, 'Listen buddy, don't you go up them stairs quiet or you're liable to be knocked in the head. You'd better call out Western Union as you go up them stairs.' So that's just what I did. I hollered Western Union all the way up the stairs. I found the man and got a good tip. I don't mind it any more, and I get the best tips over there that I get anywhere. It's those skinflints on Park Avenue that I don't like."

"Yeh, that's my experience about tips," I said. "The doorman on one of those big apartment houses just off Park Avenue called me last night and a man came out helping an old woman with a cane. He and the door man nursed her along and helped her in the cab. I drove them around about three blocks away. There was twenty cents on the clock. I put the meter on non-recording as soon as we got there so the clock wouldn't register another nickel on waiting time and cause an argument. The man and the doorman nursed the old lady out of the cab. It seemed like it took a quarter of an hour to get her out. And the man gave me a quarter and said, 'Thank you very much.'"

I turned into Park Avenue and started downtown again and the doorman at the same apartment house called me again. I thought, "'Well, I'll try one more.' It was another wealthy looking man with another crippled old woman dressed up like a million dollars. I thought they would never get her into the cab. If I was going to work that kind of trade all the time I'd get a cab with a derrick on it. And they went about three blocks too—twenty cents on the clock. I thought to myself, 'Well, by jinks, I'll leave the clock running and I'll get about fifteen cents more waiting time,' but he beat me to it. We hadn't any more than stopped when he handed me a quarter right out of the window, so I threw the flag up. He got out and got the doorman. The old lady fumbled around getting her canes ready. It took her about five minutes to make up her mind to try it. The man said, 'Now, take your time, dear; take your time. We have all the time in the world.' Yes, damn it, my time, my time."

FIRED

Harry got up a mutual benefit association for the drivers with dues of fifty cents a week to provide medical service, etc., for the men. We weren't asked to join; the fifty cents was taken out of our pay, so I stopped in at the office and said, "Harry, I'm not interested in this benefit association. I already have my own doctor and own dentist and I would rather not pay the fifty cents a week."

"Well," he said, "that's all right if you don't want it. We'll take your name off the list." Then he said, "Well, I don't know. If we let you out, why then they will all back out. I guess we'll have to let you go."

So I said, "Well, all right."

I went over to the cashier to draw my pay in full. After a few minutes Harry came over and said, "Are you married?"

"Yes."

"You got any children?"

"Yes, I got one."

He looked very upset, turned to go away, came back again and said, "I'm sorry, Hazard, but I can't help it."

THE MOGUL CHECKERS

In the meantime the Mogul Checker Taxicab Manufacturing Company had sold a lot of taxicabs in New York and they were taking the business away from everybody else. It seemed to me that it would only be a matter of time until there would be so many of them on the streets that they would be cutting each other's throats or some other cab manufacturer would come out with a new cab, dolled up to catch the public's fickle fancy, and kill them off. Cars sold for three thousand dollars, which was about twice what they were worth from a mechanical standpoint, so I thought it would be better to continue to work for somebody else. I got a job driving for a very unfortunate person who had invested in about sixty Mogul Checkers. We all worked on a percentage basis; that is the driver got thirty-five per cent of what the clock registered. Now, it was very easy to make a bargain with a passenger and leave the flag up and keep it all. The only question was how much to turn in to keep from getting fired, so I made it my business to ask the other drivers how much they booked and found that on the night line, which I was working, they varied from sixty to a hundred and fifty dollars a week. I noticed the boss kept letting out the tail enders and trying out new men, but the men who turned in better than seventy-five a week were never reached in this process. I was a pretty fair hackman and could have turned in a hundred and twenty, but I thought, "Why make the boss a present of forty-five dollars a week?" so I kept close track of it and turned in between seventy-five and eighty dollars. I made cracking good money all that year. I saved on an average of two hundred dollars a month above all living expenses.

THE DRUNKEN COP

A cop hailed me in Greenwich Village. He had a drunk with him who, he told me, was a cop too, and he wanted me to take him over to some place on Degraw Street, Brooklyn, and that he was all right.

The fellow looked rather like a cop, but I didn't like the looks of it, still I didn't see any way to get out of it, so I took him. When I got over there he climbed out of the cab in kind of a dazed condition and started walking off without offering to pay the fare, so I walked after him and told him he hadn't paid the fare yet. He opened his coat, showing a gun in a yellow holster at his hip, put his hand on it and said, "This is all the fare you'll get."

I went back to the cab and started following him with the cab. When he saw I was following him, he stepped out into the middle of the street and drew the gun. I leaned over in the seat so as to be protected by the cowl and drove the car right at him. He jumped out of the way, but I caught him a glancing blow with the mud guard and knocked him over and he dropped the gun. I stopped as quickly as possible and backed up to try and get the gun, but he got up and got the gun before I could make it, but I managed to bump him with the rear of the car again. Then he made a run to try to jump on the running board, but I stepped on the gas fast enough so that he lost his hold and fell again. He got up and started going the other way, so I backed the car, following him that way, which enabled me to use the back part of the car as a shield. When he'd stop and come at me, I'd go into low and shoot ahead a ways. We maneuvered around, up one street and down another for quite a while. Several men came out and advised me to let that guy alone, they knew him, and the best thing I could do was to forget it, but I was working for a company then and if I didn't get it I would have to pay it out of my own pocket.

He tried grabbing another taxi, but the other drivers saw the situation and got away from him. Then he got a street car and I followed it a ways. Then he gave that up and tried it on foot again. All of this time I had been looking for a cop, but none had showed up. Then I came in sight of a station house in that precinct, so I thought I would take the chance of losing him, shoot over there and get a cop.

I went in and told the sergeant about it, giving him the name that the cop had addressed him by and the fact that he carried a gun practically unconcealed. The sergeant said, "What do you expect us to do about it?"

I said, "Well, if you don't know what to do about it, I guess that settles it. So long."

He said, "Hold on there now; hold on. Who'd you say this fellow is?"

Again I gave him the name that I had heard the cop address him by and the fact that he carried a gun practically unconcealed.

"Well," he said, "now that's different. I didn't understand before he is supposed to be a cop. I don't think he could have been a cop. That's more reason for us to get after him. There's a lot of guys running around with fake badges. We got a guy the other day with a fake patrolman's badge and a fake captain's badge. You'd better go in and see one of the detectives. There's no use to put a patrolman on this. One of the detectives will bring him in."

I went into the detectives' room and told one of them about it. He had to make out a typewritten report on it. While I was talking to him, I overheard two of the others talking. One said, "I hear there was a guy got bumped off over at Murphy's yesterday. Tough luck."

The other one said, "Yeh, that's just the way it goes. I've been frisking everybody in that place day in and day out, night in and night out, and just when I get a day off something has to happen."

Well, with the report finally made out, one of the detectives went out with me to see if we could find the bird, but after a lot of walking around he decided to give it up. So I never got that two dollars and ten cents.

THE UNION

Shortly after I started with the Mogul Checkers the drivers organized a union and called a strike, demanding 40% commission, no penalties for smashing up the cars, and no firing men for low bookings. We took the owners by surprise and they had to accept our terms, ruinous as they were because they were all buying the cars on notes. I thought it was a mistake myself on the part of the drivers. It seemed a good idea to give the boss enough to keep him alive anyway. I got to stand pretty well with the boss because I didn't smash up the car—there was no profit to me in smashing up the car—and because I turned in my seventy-five regular.

Then some regular union organizers got into the union, loud-mouthed fellows who managed to hold the floor at the meetings and keep anybody else from getting a word in edgeways, who prevented the transaction of necessary business, making it necessary to call another meeting. They kept on having meetings every few days, and the real taxi drivers couldn't lay off work to go to the meetings all the time, so finally only the original leaders and the professional agitators and a few of their followers showed up, with about thirty-five men present out of a membership of four thousand. The original leaders could hardly make themselves heard, and the agitators moved for a new election of officers and elected themselves. They then proceeded to raise the dues, give themselves good salaries, hire an attorney at ten thousand a year, etc. After a few months a meeting was called to discuss a new strike in spite of the fact that we had a contract with the operators for a year. What their object was I don't know, but only about one hundred members showed up; only those in favor of striking were permitted to talk; a vote to strike was put over and a new strike was on.

It was proposed that we call the strike on the Yellow Taxicab Company as well as the others. Someone got up and objected because only one or two of the men working for the Yellows belonged to the union.

Phil O'Neil, the President of the Buckers Taxicab Association, had come to the meeting to offer his advice. He is an old timer in the game, rather old and battered looking. He got up and said, "That don't make no difference. I called a strike on the Fifth

Avenue Coach Company and five men was all I had, five men. I just had one for each entrance to the garage to hand out the strike notices in the morning. And there wasn't a bus rolled down the Avenue that day except one the Superintendent drove himself. That night the drivers all came to the meeting and joined the union."

We took his advice and declared the strike on the Yellows.

The operators were ready for us this time and didn't come to terms. After a few days the operators had the union leaders arrested for attempted extortion, and our attorney left town suddenly. The leaders issued a statement that the strike was settled satisfactorily, though we never heard what the terms were. Everybody went back to work at the old rates and nothing was ever heard of the union again. No accounting was made of the money in the treasury. No meetings were called. The president of the union started manufacturing taxicabs. It was rumored that the treasurer bought several houses in Jersey. At any rate I saw them on the street occasionally and they all looked very prosperous.

CUT RATE

Shortly after the Twentieth Century Association cut the rate from thirty cents to twenty cents a mile, the taxi meter concerns couldn't change the clocks fast enough so most of the taxicab owners who undertook to cut the rate to meet competition had to put up signs on the cabs reading twenty cents a mile and another sign inside explaining that the meter worked at thirty cents a mile and to pay the driver one-third less than the meter registered.

When the cut to twenty cents a mile was made it received a lot of publicity and people simply went crazy over riding in taxicabs, but most of them didn't seem to understand about paying one-third less than the clock registered. The company drivers had no trouble in collecting the full amount on the clock, though they had to settle with the boss for only two-thirds, out of which they still drew their forty per cent commission.

During that time I picked up a very intelligent, cultivated looking gentleman at 10th Street and Fifth Avenue who said he wanted to go to New Rochelle. He sat up on one of the little front seats so he could talk to me and asked me how I was making out at twenty cents a mile.

I said, "First rate."

"Well," he said, "I don't see much in it."

I thought of explaining the thing to him; then I decided to wait awhile.

He continued, "I take a taxi up to New Rochelle almost every night and under the old rates it always ran about six thirty or six forty. I thought that was reasonable enough. Now I got on one of the new low-rate cabs last night, and the clock registered the same six forty. I don't think there's much saving in it."

I said to myself, "Uh huh," and aloud, "Well, maybe not on a long trip." And there about a foot from his nose was the poster explaining the whole thing.

We got up there and stopped at a beautiful suburban residence. There was six seventy on the clock.

"Well, what do I owe you?" he asked, though he could see it plain enough.

"Gee, I'm worse than the other fellow. I've got six seventy."

"No," he said, "I don't think there's much saving," and he gave me seven and a half.

Out of that call I got four dollars and eighty-two cents and the boss got two dollars and sixty-eight cents. Those were great days; too bad they couldn't last forever.

THE PACKARD

The Twentieth Century cabs were getting all the business. It was disheartening driving a Mogul Checker. You would be cruising down the street and see a party you knew was looking for a cab and you would slow up in front of them and give them the sign, but they wouldn't give you a tumble. You would drive on, look back, watch them a little bit, and the first thing you know you would see a Twentieth Century come along and they would hop out in the middle of the street to hail it.

The Mogul Checker operators were in a bad way. They hadn't finished paying their notes on the cars. They looked very worried. They were skimping on repairs and trying to get by with old worn-out tires.

Up to this time you had had to have a Mogul Checker to get the business on the street though you knew it was a piece of junk, but you could get into the Twentieth Century Association with any good looking car, so I bought me a nice second-hand Packard single six for a thousand dollars cash, had it painted the Twentieth Century colors, and joined the Association, and had the swellest hack in New York for the time being. After a little while the other fellows caught on to it and there got to be more and more Packard taxis on the street. Now they are as thick as flies. I got a good day man on the job and I worked nights and altogether made about thirty dollars a day clear.

THE AGITATOR

I was up at the office of the Twentieth Century Taxicab Owners Association while we were at the height of our success with the new cut rate. While I was waiting a man came in and started to talk to the President, complaining that they didn't have meetings enough, the rank and file didn't have a chance to have a say, and it wasn't fair. I recognized this man as one of the officers who had participated in wrecking the Brotherhood of Taxicab Chauffeurs—the Mogul Checker outfit. He had evidently gone through his share. I wanted to denounce him but as I have never had any success in forcing unsolicited information on people, I contented myself with standing back and thinking of all the nice things I would like to say. How often we think of things to say when we haven't the opportunity to say them.

The President of the Association came over and said, "Hazard, you have been in this Association quite a while. Have you got anything to complain about?"

Well, there was my opportunity and I was all set. Before I got it all off my chest the union organizer had left without saying good-bye. The officers of the Twentieth Century have been friendly to me ever since.

ERRORS

I picked up an old fellow the other day who makes an interesting case for those who care for Freud's theory as to errors and for those who are thoroughly acquainted with downtown New York.

He hailed me at Seventh and Greenwich Avenues. He was a middle-aged gentleman, dressed in the style of old, old New York—black cutaway coat, striped trousers, vest with white piping around the neck, a black derby that came near being a high hat. He was just the least bit shabby, and timid.

He said, "Now, I want you to take me to that Court on Lafayette Street. Is there a Court at No. 57 Lafayette?"

"I don't know. The Criminal Court Building is near there."

"Well, take me down there. It's on Lafayette between Lexington Avenue and 3rd Street."

"Hold on," I said. "There isn't any such place."

"Well, it's somewhere in that neighborhood. Maybe it's 3rd Street between Irving Place and Lexington Avenue."

My head started to spin. "But there isn't any such place."

"Well," he said, "I'll tell you. We'll go over and inquire at that Court on Jefferson Street and Eighth Avenue."

"Wait a minute. That's another one that doesn't exist."

"Why yes. You must know that place, that big court building there at 6th Street and Tenth Avenue."

"Oh, you must mean Jefferson Market Court, right down here."

"Yes, that's it," he said, but he looked very downhearted, and added "Greenwich Street and Tenth Avenue."

"All right," I said, and I drove him to Jefferson Market Court, down to the little back door on 10th Street. In a few minutes he came out again, all smiles and bright as a daisy. "I've got it all straight now. I've got it all straight. It's No. 57 Irving Place right between 3rd Street and Lafayette."

"Hold on. I'll go in and ask him myself." As I started in, he trotted along behind me and said, "Maybe it's—" but I didn't give him a chance to give me any more.

To the desk sergeant I said, "Say, Jack, where does this bird want to go?"

He said, "Take him up to the Domestic Relations Court, 57th Street between 3rd and Lexington."

"Righto."

I started back for the cab with the old gentleman still trotting along behind me. He said, "Oh, you know him?"

"Sure."

I took the old man up to the Domestic Relations Court. He didn't seem to be a bit pleased, rather depressed, if anything. There was eighty cents on the clock. He handed me a dollar, waited for the twenty cents change, and walked off with it.

THE SCOLD

I picked up a woman at the corner of Fordham Road and Webster. She wanted to go to 180th Street and Van Nest Avenue. The cop was holding the traffic on Fordham Road.

She said, "Why don't you go ahead? I don't want to sit here all day. I'm in a hurry."

"I can't. The cop is holding the traffic."

"How's that? There's fifteen cents on the clock already."

"That's the way it works."

"Well, I won't pay it."

"You'll have to."

"Well, I'll get out."

"All right, go ahead, but you'll have to pay me the fifteen cents."

"I'll call an officer," she threatened.

"Fine. That just suits me. There's one right there," and I pointed to one standing about fifteen feet away.

By that time traffic was moving on Fordham Road and she said, "Why don't you go ahead? What's the matter with you? I never saw such a taxi driver."

We had gone about two blocks when she said, "You're going the wrong way. Don't you know where you are going?"

I slowed up. "How do you want to go?"

"Go ahead. Go ahead. Didn't I tell you I'm in a hurry."

Two blocks farther on she almost screamed, "You're going the wrong way. You're trying to run up a big bill on the clock. I won't pay it."

I put on the brake and said again, "Well, how do you want to go?"

She shouted, "Go ahead, go ahead, I'm in a hurry."

I stepped on the gas again.

She continued, "If you don't know where it is, why didn't you say so?"

"I know where it is." There is hardly any choice as to how to get there and I was going the shortest way and I knew that she must know it.

"How much is the fare going to be?" she asked.

"Oh about four dollars."

She almost choked. "You're going the wrong way. It shouldn't be more than sixty-five cents."

"Well, I wish you would tell me how you want to go. The more there is on the clock, the more I collect."

"Go on, go on. My people are waiting for me."

We kept this up all the way there.

I had sixty-five cents on the clock and she said, "I'm not going to pay you more than fifty cents. That's all it should be."

"You'll have to pay what's on the clock, and furthermore the clock is still running and it will register another nickel pretty soon and you'll have to pay that too."

She finally handed me a dollar and said, "I'm not going to give you any tip."

"That's old stuff. I knew that long ago. It's tip enough to get rid of you."

"You're the worst taxi driver I ever saw. If it weren't that my people are waiting for me I wouldn't have ridden in your old cab."

"Don't worry, they can live without you. It's a wonder to me they didn't murder you long ago."

She took a deep breath and was just starting in all over again when I went into low and let the clutch in.

POLITICAL INFLUENCE IN JERSEY

I was going up Seventh Avenue in the afternoon and I saw a party on the corner that I knew must be looking for a taxi though they hadn't hailed me. I crashed for the corner but a guy with a Luxor who had spotted them too made a quick turn around and beat me to it. I was kind of sore to lose them because it was a Bronx call; you could see they were that kind of people.

I drove on up Seventh Avenue and then four kind of half-way prosperous drunks hailed me. They looked as though I would have trouble with them but I needed the money so I stopped. Just as I expected, they wanted to go to Jersey. I drove down to the Christopher Street ferry. On the way over on the Ferry they got to racketing around in the cab and broke one of the windows, so I said to them, "Please understand right now that you have got to pay for that window."

One of them says, "What window?"

Another one, "We didn't break any window."

A third, "That window was broke when we got in the cab. Where do you get that stuff? We ain't going to pay for any window. Nah, you're all wrong."

They kept on that way until the Ferry pulled into the slip in New Jersey and I drove off. Then one of them says, "You got to remember you're in Jersey now. You ain't in your own town. We know everybody over here. We got a strong drag with the politicians here. I'm a personal friend of the Police Commissioner."

Another one said, "I stand right in with the crowd."

Another one said, "Nah, you're out of luck collecting for that window. That window was broke when we got in the cab."

I said to myself, "Well, we'll see, we'll see." So I drove on along in the direction of their destination. Bye and Bye I spotted a police station and there was a driveway right into the building, so I turned sharp and drove right in and I came to a door in the building and through it I could see the sergeant sitting at his desk, so I pulled up and walked in and told the sergeant about it.

In the meantime the four passengers followed me in and told the sergeant all about it, they didn't have anything to do with that broken window and they didn't know anything about it, and they pulled out letters and things to show him how important they were.

He listened to all they had to say and then he walked out with me and looked at the window and asked me what it would cost to have it fixed. He looked at the clock to see what was on the clock.

I told him the window would cost me five dollars and there was a dollar and a half on the clock and there was a dollar ferriage.

So he says, "That makes seven fifty altogether."

"Yes," I said.

"Is that the least you can get that window fixed for?"

"Well, I might shade it a little bit, but that's about what it would come to."

He goes back to his desk and says, "Well, gentlemen, as I understand it, you owe this man seven dollars and fifty cents, and if you don't pay him I will have to lock you up."

So they dug down into their pockets immediately and came across with the seven fifty, and the sergeant says, "I don't think you had better take these fellows any farther; let them walk the rest of the way."

"Personal friends of the chief of police," says I to myself.

SMOKING

I picked up a woman on Fifth Avenue to go somewhere on Park Avenue. While I was waiting in traffic I lit a cigarette. She said, "How dare you light a cigarette while I am riding in this cab? Don't you realize that it is an insult to me, that that isn't a properly respectful attitude?"

I said, "Why, madam, I don't know what to make of this. I really didn't intend any offense. Most of the women want to know if I have a match. I've thought of quitting smoking when I have passengers in the cab to keep the women from borrowing all my cigarettes. They hardly ever give the matches back until I ask for them, and they hardly ever remember when it comes to the tip. But this is the first kick I ever had except as to the brand of cigarettes I smoke."

She laughed then and said she really didn't mind, and she gave me a good tip when we got there.

INSURANCE

Along about 1921 a law was passed requiring taxicab owners to give bond for the payment of damage claims against them that might result from accidents. Most of the hack drivers assumed that the law was passed to make business for the insurance companies because the law was so worded that no individual could give bond but had to pay some large concern to give bond for him. The law said that a bond must be given for twenty-five hundred dollars for payment of damages for each person injured, so you couldn't put up a twenty-five-hundred-dollar bond because there was no way of computing how many people might be injured. The thoroughly solvent old insurance companies, of course, wouldn't handle the business, so fly-by-night concerns were set up for the purpose. They charged forty-five dollars a month to furnish bond. There was great indignation and the City authorities didn't seem disposed to put themselves out to enforce it, so we worked most of the next year without bothering with bonds. Then the State authorities contrived means of enforcing it through the State License Bureau by revoking anybody's license who let his bond lapse.

I think the immediate effect of the law was to cause more accidents, because the independent driver, having paid his forty-five dollars, felt like getting something for his money. Furthermore, if you rammed another car, you could sit back and smile and say, "I am insured." The companies were not inclined to fire drivers on account of accidents because they were covered by insurance. The principal disadvantage of having an accident was the time lost.

Most of the companies that were organized for the business paid their officers very large salaries and in one way or another managed to go broke without paying very many damage claims, so that out of the premiums that the taxicab owners had paid in, very little went to the victims of accidents.

The Twentieth Century Association formed a mutual insurance company and reduced the rate to twenty-four dollars a month, but the State Insurance Commission compelled them to raise the rate to twenty-eight dollars a month in spite of the fact that they had built up a large surplus and wanted to further reduce the rates. Possibly the Commission was afraid that the private insurance companies would be pushed overboard. The buckers, the Amalgamated Taxi Owners Association, organized a mutual in a somewhat different way and succeeded in reducing the premium to about fifteen dollars a month, while maintaining a large surplus. The Companies reduced the rate to thirty dollars a month and continued to go broke one after another.

The Twentieth Century and the Amalgamated had a great advantage in that their officers are old experienced taxi drivers and realized that the owner driver is the best risk because he is experienced and has more at stake, and they are in a position to get the owner driver business.

Having fleeced the taxicab owners under the pretense of protecting the dear public, some of the politicians at the last election organized mass meetings for hack drivers and attempted to swing the taxicab vote by making impassioned speeches about how unjustly the hackmen had been treated under the bonding law which operated against them and against nobody else, and proposed to pass a new law compelling owners of private cars and trucks to carry bond too; in other words, we have tramped on you; now you get revenge by helping us tramp on everybody else. I don't know whether it worked or not.

GOOD INTENTIONS

It was the last day of the month and I was cruising down from the Bronx to pay my monthly insurance premium at the Twentieth Century Association because I wouldn't be able to work on the first if I didn't have the receipt to stick on the wind shield. I had to turn down a call to Brooklyn in order to get there in time.

While the girl was making out the receipt I said, "It's so much better to get down here a few days in advance instead of having to rush the last minute."

She said, "Yes, and then you can have the receipt mailed to you instead of having to go over to the License Bureau and wait there in line for it."

"Yes," I said, "it's so much better and then you can get it off your mind and don't have to worry about it. If you let it go until the last minute you have to rush down here and have to turn down business. It's so much better to pay it ahead of time."

She said, "Yes, you don't have to wait your turn here if you come early. There's always such a rush the last few days."

I said, "Yes, I always figure to get down here and get the premium paid at least a week in advance—but I never have."

PERSEUS

I remember reading about a Greek named Perseus who planted some dragon's teeth. A crowd of tough-looking soldiers sprouted up out of the ground, all armed and looking for trouble. Perseus was afraid he couldn't handle them so he hid and threw rocks at them. They fell to fighting amongst themselves. And when they were thinned out and tired enough, Perseus stepped out and took charge of them.

New York ain't such a bad town after all.

I picked up a call at 28th and Ninth for Grand Central. He asked me if I could make it by 4:35. I said I didn't know but I would try. It was 4:15.

I cut through 28th to get the worst over first. Well, one of those one-horse mail wagons, doing about two and a half miles an hour, got in front of me. Those wagons are wide and by holding the middle of the open space, he kept me from passing. Where there was a gap at the curb, he would shake the horse up enough to keep me from passing. I finally beat him to it on the third try and was going on the button when a woman stepped out in front of me. She could see me but knew I had to stop and figured I was able. People sure have a lot of faith in chauffeurs. I came close enough to make her jump, but she went on with her nose in the air and waggling her rear end wicked.

I got across Eighth with a clear road and the lights with me at Seventh. I gave her all she had on the chance I could beat the light. The light flashed just as I started across, and a Mack truck started on the jump and cut me off. Had to slide and turn to keep from ramming him. Those trucks have it all over you; you can't hurt the damn truck and they know it.

Good luck after the light changed and I was shooting up Fourth Avenue. A Ford truck was trying to beat me to an opening when a woman stepped in front of him. Just as he slapped on the brake, one rear wheel hit some manure, and he might as well not have had any brakes. He caught her right square—kerwham—and bent the radiator.

Made Grand Central with two minutes to spare. The man seemed very pleased and gave me a two-dollar tip.

YOU COULDN'T BLAME HIM

There is a very capable traffic cop at Spring and Lafayette. A big husky fellow and very alert and energetic. If you want to take a left turn at his corner you can get out in the middle and give him the signal a half a block away and by the time you get down to him, nine times out of ten, he will have spotted a gap for you and hold up his hand and motion you to take it on the fly.

I was driving down there the other day with a party in the cab and a couple of Sunday drivers got in front of me and I had to take the middle to pass them just above Spring. The cop saw me and thought I wanted to turn left. I signaled him straight ahead but he didn't get it.

He opened up a gap for me and signaled me to shoot it and stepped over to the right to give me room. I couldn't get by him on the right and had to stop. He kept holding the traffic and motioning me to take the turn, and when it dawned on him that I did not want to turn and didn't intend to, he put his hands on his hips and gave me a terrible look. "Pull over there."

I pulled over to the curb.

"Where's your book."

I handed it to him.

"What's the matter with you?"

I said, "God damn it, I've been passing you here day in and day out for six years and we never had any trouble before."

He handed the book back. "Get the hell out of here."

I got.

POCKET BOOKS

At first I made a practice of returning articles left in the cab, but I soon got over that. Most people showed very little appreciation and the time lost was money out of my pocket. I found a pair of glasses in the cab. They looked very expensive; the frames were of silver or platinum filigree work. They weren't worth much to me, but they might be worth a lot to the owner. I happened to remember the woman they belonged to and the apartment house I took her to way up Broadway. I drove up there and described the woman to the doorman and he phoned her and got permission to send me up. When I got up there the woman acted as though I had stolen the glasses. So unless the people look right I don't bother.

I heard a man and his son about ten years old discussing this matter in the back of the cab. The boy said, "If a taxi-driver finds something in the cab and doesn't return it that isn't right, is it Papa?"

"Well, yes and no, son; that depends. If he found a sum of money, say a thousand dollars, why he might have use for that money, but if he found a fur piece, say, it wouldn't be of much use to him even though it cost a thousand dollars and he couldn't sell it for much. Now if he returned it the owner could afford to pay him a reward that would be more than he could sell it for."

"You mean, like the time Mama left her fur coat in a cab and the driver brought it back?"

"Yes, son."

After quite a while the boy said, "Mama gave him two dollars."

I am always finding women's pocket books in the cab. I brought so many pocket books home to my little daughter that she doesn't know what to do with them all. One time I had a couple of cars so that I had drivers working for me, and they started bringing home pocket books to my little girl. We had pocket books all over the place.

It's funny they all contained about the same things. The description of one about fits them all: From five to thirty cents; a handkerchief; some sticks of chewing gum with some portions of sticks, the labels carefully folded over the ends; a mirror; lip sticks; rouge; powder puff; a rosary; and a small bottle of bichloride of mercury tablets. One contained a Christmas list:

Uncle Tom—Necktie.
Father—Socks.
Cousin Jim—Necktie.
Ben—Necktie.
Grandpa—Socks.
Mother—Handkerchiefs.
Aunt Lilly—Handkerchiefs.
Mary—Stockings.
Gene—Stockings.

And one contained a list of words, followed by definitions:

Exquisite—Expensive.
Refined— ————.
Hectic—A disease.
Virgin—Young.
Control—When you are experienced.
Selfish—When an old man takes you to a matinée.

Now, I don't know that all women's pocket books are like this, but I do know that this is the kind that is left in taxicabs.

HACK MEN

There are all kinds of people driving hacks in New York. There are a lot of gunmen, gorillas, etc., who serve a district leader at election time and get a certain amount of protection in turn, and who drive taxicabs as a convenient side line. Most of them are to be found on what are called closed lines; that is, some places where taxicabs stand in line for business at a designated hack stand, a tough gang will get together and hold the line for themselves and keep outsiders out.

At the other extreme there is a close relative of the late Elbert Hubbard who has been hacking in New York ever since automobiles came in, and he can tell some very good stories if you happen to meet him in one of the Coffee Pots about three o'clock in the morning.

Then there is George Mast. His people have followed the sea for generations. He was a Captain in the Merchant Marine before the War. During the War he was given a commission in the Navy. He had a couple of supply ships blown out from under him, one right after the other, just off New York Harbor. He was then placed in command of a destroyer and was Captain in the service after the War. One day he received orders by wireless direct from the Navy Department to call in at Bermuda and pick up ten cases of special ammunition. He thought they were funny looking ammunition cases, but there was nothing to do but obey orders. When he got into New York Harbor, the prohibition officers boarded the ship at quarantine, seized the ten cases of special ammunition which proved to be a fine assortment of wines and liqueurs from France.

George was kept out of jail but was retired from the service on half pay pending an investigation. The papers in the case were supposed to have been forwarded to Washington. The case was never officially investigated.

George is, as he describes himself, "fair, fat and forty," but he manages to get by driving a taxi, as his half pay is hardly enough to support his family.

Once a month he drives down to the Navy boat landing at South Ferry, parks the car, takes off the old tin hack badge, strides up to the orderly in charge of the landing. The orderly salutes and he salutes. George says, "Take me to the Island." The launch is manned and they take him to the Island where he is received as a Captain for the moment again, draws his half pay, returns to South Ferry, puts the old tin badge on and goes back to hacking.

THE BAD GUY

I met Capt. Mast and he told me this one:

"I picked up a tough-looking guy late at night to go away out near Coney Island. I wouldn't have taken him but it was a dull night and I didn't like to lose the money. After we got over the bridge he started talking like this, 'You're going to get the run of your life to-night. You're going to have a sweet time getting that dough off me.' At first I thought he was joking; then I thought he was a little bit drunk. He kept right on with that talk and finally I saw he meant it. He said, 'You guys think you are tough.' I said, 'Oh, I'm no fighter. Us hack drivers get a hard name but most of us can't scrap much.' I thought that would pacify him a little, but he kept right on worse than ever until I got pretty near out there. Then I spotted a police booth along the Parkway, so I ran right up close to it, then slapped on the brake hard and said, 'Just a minute, buddy, I got a friend of mine I want to speak to here,' and I pulled the cab up right in front of the police booth. The cop came out and I told him I had a passenger who refused to pay the fare. In the meantime the man had got out the door on the other side and was running across the street. The cop jumped on the running board and we went after him. When he saw us coming he stopped running. The cop said, 'Why don't you pay this man his fare?' The fellow said, 'I don't owe him any fare; I wasn't in his cab.'

"The cop said, 'Go on. What are you running for?' and grabbed him by the coat and swung him around towards the cab.

"The man said, 'You can't get rough with me. What proof you got?'

"Bang. The cop hit him right square in the mouth and knocked him backward into the open door of the cab. He hopped on the running board and said, 'Drive over to the station house.'

"The passenger said. 'Never mind. I'll pay him. What you got on the clock, you——?'

"I said, 'Two dollars seventy cents.'

"He pulled out three dollars, handed it to me and said, 'Give me thirty cents, you——you.'

"The cop cuffed him alongside the head, but he waited and got his thirty cents and walked off with it."

PROHIBITION AGENTS

Another time George told me this one:

"I got a guy who claimed to be a prohibition agent who wanted to follow another car. We followed the car way out on Long Island and back again. He told me there would be a big tip in it if I kept the other car in sight, and I certainly had to step on the gas. I may be fair, fat and forty, but I showed them what a fat man can do. The guy talked so much about the big tip that I got kind of suspicious. When I got back to New York, stopped over on Greenwich Street, I had twelve dollars on the clock. He took out a twenty and said, 'Have you got change?' and hung on to the bill. I saw I was due to be skunked, so I said, 'Yes, I got change,' and I pulled out a fistful of ones, reached over and got the twenty out of his hand. In the meantime I shoved the transmission lever into second with my knee, and as soon as I got hold of that twenty I stepped on the gas and let the clutch in. That old bus fairly leaped off the ground."

BEN LINDSAY

I have been reading this stuff by Ben Lindsay about sex. I really can't see anything more complicated about the sex business than about the business of buying an automobile.

I like a Packard. I had one that I drove about two hundred and sixty-eight thousand miles. I took care of it, and it never failed me. If I had to get out of a tight place, I could step on the gas, and I knew just what she would do, and she always did it. Owning that Packard to me meant being sure of having the car I liked best, having the exclusive use of it, being sure that no irresponsible person who had no stake in it would put it out of order, being able to take care of it and know that somebody else wouldn't bang it all up. Now if that old Packard could talk I don't imagine that it would resent the fact that I thought I owned it because it would realize that in so far as I owned it, it also owned me, and I think it would have been rather proud of the fact that it was worth owning.

People who have a lot of money don't have to worry so much about buying a car. If they don't like the first one, they can get a second one; but for ordinary folks it is different.

Maybe a man would like to have a Buick. He feels he would be perfectly satisfied with a Buick. But he hasn't money enough to buy one. Now if he goes and buys a Chevrolet on the installment plan, what with the expense of keeping up the Chevrolet, he may never get money enough to get a Buick.

Some people like to buy a Chevrolet or a Dodge on the installment plan. After they have worn the new off of it, they stop making payments and let it be taken away from them.

There are some people of means who like to have a Ford because they don't have to worry about it. If it gets smashed up, they can get another one. A second-hand one can be had for next to nothing.

Then there are some people who prefer to ride in taxis. Of course, you can't expect much in a taxi. A lot of them are all battered up. As like as not, the previous passenger has spit all over the floor and scattered cigarette butts around. But you can get one whenever you want it, pay the fare when you get there, and you are through with it. Or if anything happens to it, you just pay what's on the clock, and get another one.

On the other hand there are some people that like to have a Packard or a Pierce Arrow or a Rolls Royce. They would rather get what they want, stick to it, and keep it in good shape. They don't see any fun in riding around in other people's Fords.

Now Bertrand Russell says jealousy should not be considered a virtue any more, but if you go monkeying around with somebody's Packard for which he has paid good money and thinks highly of, why you are likely to get a busted nose and that's all there is to it.

VAIT FOR 'EM

I was playing the Chatham line one Tuesday night when business was dull. The drivers all gathered up around one of the cabs and got to talking. One said he had a good waiting call. Another said, "Waiting call. You don't know anything about good waiting calls. Listen to this one. Remember last Wednesday it was raining? I was on day shift and I picks this guy up in the mornin', big, swell-lookin' guy, and he keeps me the whole day, just short runs and waitin'. Along in the afternoon he goes into a swell apartment house. Well, I waited an hour and I commenced to get worried so I goes in and asks the elevator man if he knows this guy. He says, 'Sure, he's all right. His name's Klein; he's here right along.' So I goes back and sits in the cab; smokin' cigarettes; and the rain drizzlin' down steady, and I waits another hour. Then I goes in and asks the telephone operator to call this guy up and ask him if he wants the cab to wait any longer. He says, 'Tell him to wait; I want him to wait.'

"Well, half past four come and I was supposed to be in the garage by four, but I didn't know what to do so I called up the boss and told him about it and asked him what to do. The boss is a Jew. He says, 'You ah gattING a dollAH end a hef an ouAH end die cah is stendING? VAIT for him! VAIT for him! If it is rainING go inSIDE; get a cup COFFee but VAIT for him! VAIT for him! Get in die bek of die ceb: mek yourself comfortable but VAIT for him! VAIT for him!'

"I got in the cab and waited and waited. Six o'clock come and seven o'clock, and the meter was clicking right along. I got out and wound it up once in a while. Nine o'clock come and there was thirty-five dollars on the clock, and I gets worried again so I has the telephone operator call him up again. He says, 'You tell him I want him to wait for me; if he's scared of his money, I'll pay him now. But I want him to wait for me.'

"I told the doorman I'd pay for the coffee and sandwiches for the bunch if he would go and get 'em, so I minded the door and he went and got lunch for us. Then I crawled back in the cab and took a nap for a while. I was scared to call him up any more for fear he'd get sore.

"He never came out until seven o'clock the next mornin'. He was lookin' terrible. He had a girl with him. 'Now,' he says, 'I want you to drive me over to Tiffany's because I want to buy my sweetie some jewelry.' Well, we drives down Fifth Avenue and stops in front of Tiffany's, and they ain't open yet, so we waits there and the cop was givin' us the eye. He looked terrible. Finally they opened the store and they starts to go in and the doorman won't let 'em in. Oh, he looked terrible. He pulls out the roll and the doorman lets him in then. Then the clerks wasn't goin' to wait on him, until he gets the roll out, and then he got service.

"After that he drops the girl off at the apartment house and I takes him up to New Rochelle. What a call!

"Well, that wasn't all there was to it. You see, this guy was one of the big men in the Mongoose Taxi Manufacturing Company and the boss said that Goldberg, you know, the head salesman, called up about it. Well, the next day this Goldberg comes over when I am turnin' in and the boss says he wanted me to take him over to the Astor, and for me to take him, the night man can wait. Goldberg got in and I started off with him. He sat on one of the little seats so he could talk to me. He says, 'Did you have a party named Klein Wednesday?'

"I says, 'That I couldn't say. Maybe I did. Maybe I didn't.'

"He says, 'I'm the head salesman of the Mongoose Taxi Manufacturing Company. What I say goes with your boss. I can have you fired.'

"I says, 'Well, maybe you can and maybe you can't.'

"He says, 'You rode that man around all day, didn't you?'

"I says. 'Maybe I did and maybe I didn't.'

"He says, 'You took him down to the ———— Apartment House didn't you?'

"I says, 'I couldn't say. Maybe I did and maybe I didn't.'

"Then he says, 'Where did you take him from there?'

"I says, 'I couldn't say.'

"He kept at me all the way over to the Astor and then he told me to wait for him. I didn't want to wait for him, so in about half an hour I tells the doorman to find out if he wanted me to wait and if not to get the money. The doorman came back and gave me six dollars and a half. He said the guy didn't want me to wait and asked him how much was on the clock so he says six dollars and a half. I only had a buck twenty on the clock so I offered to split it with him, but he didn't want nothin'.

"Well, the next day the boss said that Goldberg had complained that I overcharged him. I said I didn't overcharge him and the boss says, 'Whaddayu mean you didn't overcharge him?' wouldn't tell him no more than that I didn't overcharge him. Well, that night this Goldberg was back again and he says, 'You're the fresh taxi driver that charged me six dollars and a half to take me over to the Astor, and you wouldn't give me no information.'

"I says, 'Did you give me six dollars and a half?'

"'Well, no,' he said, 'I gave it to the doorman.'

"'Well,' I said, 'You'd better talk to the doorman.'

"So him and the boss got in the cab and we goes over to the Astor again. The same doorman was on, you know, that big Irishman. Goldberg says to him, 'Did this man tell you there was six dollars and a half on the clock when he was waiting for me yesterday?'

"The doorman says, 'And who arrh you to be askin' me quistions? Whaht authority have you got?'

"'Well,' says Goldberg, 'I just wanted to know.'

"'Well,' says the doorman, 'if it's any satisfaction to yuh he didn't tell me nothin' whaht was on the clock. I told yuh there was six fifty on the clock and you paid me six fifty, and what I done with the six fifty is me own business, and what was on the clock I don't know. End is thir iny more quistions yud like to ask?'

"I drove them back to the garage and the boss says to Goldberg, 'You didn't pay the driver. There's a dollar forty on the clock,' so Goldberg paid me the dollar forty."

SWEET CAPS

I was standing with the flivver taxi at Sixth Avenue and 4th Street late one night hoping to pick up a couple of stray uptowners too drunk to get home on the subway. I saw a couple coming but they didn't look like business. They weren't drunk and, though the girl was all dressed up, she looked rather thin and worried and the man was little and shabby. They stopped alongside of the cab and looked me over.

The girl said, "Are you working? I may have a job for you in a little while."

"Sure. I'll be here."

She looked across the street and following her glance I saw a well-dressed man, well lit.

She said to her companion, "That John looks like a live one. Wait here." And she crossed the street.

He took a quick look up and down the street and seemed satisfied and said, "How's business?"

"Tough."

"Nobody's got any money since the war's over."

"I used to make good jack in the shipyards," I said, "but they're all shut down now. I saved some money and bought this hack when things got bad."

"Did you work in the shipyards too? Christ, it was good, wasn't it? I was bucking up before the war so I got right on rivetin'. What dough we made. Twelve and fifteen cents on shell! I got as much as ten cents on buttonsets in the intercostals."

"Too bad the war didn't last forever, hey."

"I saved up a big stake but I lost it. I bought a gin mill and cabaret down here but yuh can't make no money at it. Yuh have to slip it all as fast as yuh make it and when yuh can't come across with all they want, they break yuh."

As he talked he kept a sharp lookout. He looked to me to be pretty small for a riveter. Riveting is hard heavy work but a few small men make good at it; some of the best I've ever seen. They don't last long at it though. The strain breaks them down in a few years. I'm big and strong, but my right arm started to go dead and numb after five years with the hammer.

The girl returned looking discouraged. "He's too far gone," she said. "The booze they sell now is sumpin terrible." Then to him, "Got a cigarette?"

"No, that was the last one."

She rummaged around in her purse for some time and handed him a coin. "You can get a pack of Sweet Caps."

He walked over to the drug store and she said, "I never saw business so bad. And the cops,—my God. I'm just after doing thirty days in Bedford."

I said, "There was a lush here last night you coulda had; too bad you weren't around."

"Think of that. And I didn't get a thing all last night."

"Have you got a room?"

"No, you can't use no room on account of the cops. I always get a taxi. I tell 'em the taxi is five bucks. Of course, if he won't pay the driver that much, I make up the difference myself."

The man returned and they lit their cigarettes. "Here comes one, maybe," the man said. "I'll look him over." He hurried off.

"He's a prince of a fellow. He usta make big money but his health gave out. He ain't strong enough for that shipyard work. He spent a lot on me." Her thin, tense face looked very wistful.

The man came back looking hopeful. "I think you can get that John."

She powdered her nose and hurried off.

He posted himself to watch and said, "She's a great kid. I met her in the cabaret before I bought it. I spent a pile of dough on her. She's made a lot of money. She don't spend no time on 'em at all. Just long enough to get her hooks on that fifteen bucks, and out they go."

The girl returned dejected. "He's no good. Lookin' for charity,—them damned school teachers."

"Here comes a dick," the man said.

"Did he spot us yet?"

"No."

"So long buddy," they said and hurried off.

TRAINING 'EM

Mack used to play the Union Square hotel when it was a closed line. He was a little guy but darn well put together. He was no good with his hands on account of his nose. He had a glass nose. Any kind of punch in the nose practically put him out. That was what made him dangerous. He couldn't afford to take chances. He had two very mean tricks. If a bloke hit at him he'd grab him by the wrist with both hands and turn around and bring the arm down on his shoulder, elbow down, and either break the arm or throw the guy over his shoulder and land him on his head on the sidewalk. If he missed the wrist he would get the guy by the chin and the back of the head and twist his head quick and hard. It don't sound like much but just let somebody that knows how to do it try it on you.

He broke a man's neck that way once and came near getting into trouble over it. On account of there not being any marks on him and his having had a few drinks the cops thought the booze killed him.

He was kind of touchy too, wouldn't stand for a passenger bawling him out. He put a woman out of the cab once for looking at him through one of them lorgnettes. She took his number and reported him to the police but it turned out all right. You see, his hack license had been suspended for something so he had borrowed my book and badge and she took the badge number. Well, of course, I got the summons, and when I appeared before the commissioner she said I wasn't the man because I'm about twice as big as Mack so I told her she must have made a mistake in the number. She said it was very strange.

I was talking about getting a job driving private and Mack said he used to drive private. I asked him how he liked it. He said, "It's all right if you can get a good job, but they're hard to get. The best thing is to get a boss that ain't used to having a chauffeur and break him in right and then watch your step and you're all right.

"I used to drive for Harrison, the big corporation lawyer. They were terrible at first; driving from the back seat. I couldn't stand it. They got so bad on a tour through Massachusetts once that I got out and left the car in the middle of the road about half way between two towns and walked to the railroad and came back to New York. The old man followed me—he weighs about three hundred pounds and isn't any taller than me and said, 'William, now William, I think we ought to be able to come to an understanding. But I was too mad to talk.

"I got a letter from him in a couple of weeks asking me to come back to work and I went back and we got along all right."

I said, "Well, how did he get to be such a big lawyer?"

"Oh he was there. He didn't know anything else, but he knew the Law. Several big corporations paid him about fifty thousand dollars apiece just to advise them. He hardly ever went into court but when he did he acted like Supreme Court judges were dirt under his feet. Oh he was there.

"I made fifty dollars a week and pickings. I got a three hundred split from the salesman when he bought a new car. He kept a Dodge to run around in and a big car to tour in and go out at night. I'd go around and see who I could get the best terms out of. Then I'd say to the old man, 'This car is getting in pretty bad shape.'

"He'd say, 'Why, William,—a—it seems to be running all right.'

"I wouldn't say anything, and then in a couple of days he'd say, 'Well, William,—a—what do you think—a—is wrong with the car?'

"I'd say, 'You might not notice it; it sounds good yet, but before long it will give trouble; the pistons are bad and the universals are working loose and there's a click in the rear end like a broken tooth.'

"He said, 'Maybe I'd better—a—turn it in—a—while I can get something for it.'

"We bought Cadies three years and the agency thought they could go without me then and wouldn't give me any commission so the next year the old man bought a Pierce and that taught them a lesson. We got a Cady again next year. A Cady is better for big fat people. A Packard is all right for tall thin people.

"I certainly earned my money and I needed it then. I was married then and my wife could spend it. I got a rake off on the gas and tires and garage and when the boss went touring he gave me five dollars for dinner and hotel bill and I slept in the car and ate in lunch wagons, but I never had a dollar to spare.

"The missus was just as big as the boss. She liked to drive out in the country days and tramp around. I drove the Dodge on those trips. She picked the roughest, narrowest roads she could find and when we couldn't get any farther with the car, she'd get out and walk. Then she'd climb over the rocks till she'd get some place she couldn't get down from and then she'd holler, 'William, William, I can't get down; come and help me.'

"She got started sliding down a rock once. She hollered, 'William, I'm slipping.' I got hold of her around the waist, but I couldn't hold her; she weighs about three hundred pounds. I got my feet hooked around a tree and stopped her but she damn near pulled me in two. She said, 'William, what shall I do? I can't get up.' I said, 'Turn around and get ahold of me and climb up and get ahold of the tree and then I'll climb up and get ahold of the next one, and we can get back that way.'

"She had a kitten she used to carry around in the car. One time she had me stop on Fifth Avenue alongside the park and let the kitten out on the grass to play. A dog came along and chased the kitten up a tree. I chased the dog away but the kitten wouldn't come down so the missus said, 'William, can't you climb the tree and get her down?' I climbed the tree and got the kitten down and it scratched hell out of me.

"Well, we drove down Fifth Avenue and stopped at Lord and Taylor's and the doorman opened the door and she got out. Then she said, 'William, William, I'm caught.' I looked around and there she was with her back to the car and her feet not quite touching the sidewalk. I got out and saw that she had stepped out onto the running board and leaned back against the car and got the front door hinge hooked into her corset strings behind and when she stepped off the running board the corset string stretched almost enough to let her down almost to the sidewalk. I tried to lift her, but she was so heavy and hard to get a hold of that I couldn't raise her high enough to get her unhooked. Finally the doorman lifted from one side and me from the other and we got her off.

"They liked to go places on the train and have me meet them there with the big car. The boss would say, 'William, we're going to Boston to-night. Will you—a—take us down to Grand Central and then—a—drive up to Boston and—a—meet the train in the morning?' Then in a couple of days I'd have to take them to the depot in Boston and meet the train again in New York.

"They did a lot of touring to Florida and Los Angeles and so on. They liked to talk to their friends about it. We'd start out for Los Angeles and about the second morning when I'd call at the hotel for them the boss would say, 'William,—a—we have to call on some friends here to-day. You—a—go on in the car and we'll—a—take a Pullman tonight and—a—meet you in Chicago to-morrow so as—a—not to delay you.' Well, it would be like that all the way. They couldn't stand more than one or two days touring at a time.

"One time in Washington the boss said, 'William,—a—why is it that we never get any service in the hotels like other people?' I said, 'Give them tips enough and you'll get service.'

"He said, 'Well, William,—a—how much do you think I should give them?'

"I said, 'Give the doorman a five-dollar bill when you come and the same when you leave. Then you don't have to tip him every time you go in or out. Then give the head bell hop . . .'

"He said, 'Well—a—William—a—suppose I give you the money? Could you arrange it for me? How much will you need?'

"I said, 'Well forty dollars will be enough if you're only staying a week.'

"He said, 'All right, here's fifty.'

"I said to the doorman, 'My people want service and they'll pay for it. They're regular. Here's five dollars and there'll be as much more when we leave.'

"He said, 'That's O. K. with me.'

"Then I fixed things up with the others. Well, they got more service than the King and Queen of England after that The missus was tickled pink. She smiled all over. The boss said, 'This is fine. William. How in the world did you manage it?'

"They had a hard time keeping cooks and maids. One day the missus said, 'William, maybe you could get us a cook and a maid.' I went down to the employment office and looked over the people there. There was a couple that looked like they knew their stuff so I told them about the job and they said they'd take a chance. They got along fine. The man cooked and his wife waited on tables and helped around.

"I made all the repairs on the cars. The missus took a lot of interest in it. She used to come out to the garage back of the house and watch me grinding valves and wanted to learn all about it.

She bragged to visitors about it. I'd go in to get my orders and she'd say to her guests, 'William does all our repair work. You're grinding the cylinders today, aren't you, William?' I'd say, 'Yes, ma'am,' and keep a straight face and most of the guests didn't know the difference anyway.

"Old ex-President McBust used to visit them a good deal. He and the old man were a tight fit on the back seat of the Cady. I took them out to the country club one afternoon and they stayed till nine-thirty P. M. I had a date in town for ten P. M., so when they finally came out I stepped on the gas to try and get back in time. I had the bus doing seventy-five when the old man says, 'A—William—a—aren't you going rather—a—fast?'

"I says, 'Why no—not particularly.'

"After about five minutes he says, 'But William—a—it seems to me that you're going rather—a—fast. Possibly I'm mistaken but it seems to me that you're going—a—rather fast.'

"I said, 'Well, that's probably due to your condition.'

"After a while he said, 'A—William—am I as bad off as all that?'

"I said, 'Well—pretty bad.'

"When I got them home they staggered when they got out of the car though they had walked perfectly straight when they came out of the country club. They helped each other up the stairs and I never heard any complaint about the speeding.

"I didn't have much work to do one winter and a bootlegger got me to make a trip once in a while at night. It didn't interfere with driving for Harrison. The bootlegger had a big Pierce tuned up to a hair. You could do seventy down a rough road as smooth as a whistle. A guard went with me and we ran about a hundred miles along the Sound and got loaded up so as to start back about two A. M. and get in before daylight. We got chased and shot at a couple of times, but we just walked off and left them. I got fifty dollars a trip and made about two trips a week. They put the car in the shop after each trip and kept it tuned up perfect.

"Well, the prohibition agents or the hijackers must have laid for us as one night they cut loose on us with what sounded like a machine gun. I slid down to the floor boards and drove with one hand on the wheel and one hand on the throttle—I couldn't get my feet on the control on the pedals in that position—and just peeked out over the edge of the cowl and kept the throttle to the floor board. The other fellow got down on the floor boards too and got his hands on the clutch and brake pedals so as to work them if necessary. They must have had a gun set high because it was all going into the load at the top. The load protected us and none of the tires got hit. We got away from them in short order, but it was hell while it lasted.

"After we had got well away we were so shaky we stopped to get a bottle out of the load and have a bracer. We went through half of the load of sixty cases before we found an unbroken quart. Booze was dripping all over the road under the car.

"When we got into town right near the boss's house the motor commenced to sputter like the gas wasn't feeding right and I had to go into second, and we just crawled along. Then we saw the police car coming toward us down the street. We didn't dare meet it because you could smell the car a block away, so I told the other fellow, 'I'll drive the car into the old man's garage and we will leave it there until I get it fixed up enough to get through.

"We had a four-car garage on the old man's place with two doors so you could put two cars on each side, one behind the other. I didn't think they were going to use the Dodge the next day so I put the Pierce behind the Dodge so I could get out with the Cady. I couldn't turn the lights on without being seen from the house so I figured to fix the Pierce the next day and get it out the next night. I had a room upstairs over the garage so I turned in to get some sleep.

"Well, about eight o'clock the phone rang. The missus said she had got a telegram; guests were coming; she would have to go to the depot to meet them. She said to drive the Dodge. She always liked to drive the Dodge. I told her I was doing some repair work on the Dodge and it wasn't ready to run and I would have to use the Cady.

"Well, we drove down and picked up the guests, two Anti-saloon League leaders and their wives. When we got back old McBust had come over to have breakfast with them.

"I went out to the garage and went to work on the Pierce. It was a sight. There was half a dozen holes in the upper part of the gas tank and I guess some dirt or chips had got into the gas line and clogged it.

"In about an hour the phone rang again and the missus said to come to the house. When I got there they were all sitting around at the breakfast table and the missus said, 'William, we all want to drive out to Greenwich and come back in time for a matinee. Will you be able to make the trip and get back in time?' And then before I answered, she said to the guests, 'William does all our repair work. William, what are you doing to the car now?'

"I said, 'Oh, I'm just taking up the play in the rear end.'

"The missus said, 'It's so interesting to watch William working on the car. I am learning all about it. He takes up on the pistons and scrapes the crankshaft and everything. Let's all go out and see how he is getting along. Wouldn't you like to see the inside of the machine?'

They all said, 'Why yes, it would be very interesting,' and got up.

"I said, 'You'd better not come out now; everything is all dirty out there and you will get your clothes all dirty.'

"They said, 'Oh, that's all right, William. We're used to roughing it.'

"I near went crazy trying to shoo them back to the house, but I couldn't stop them. They just kept right on coming.

"Well, they took one look at that old Pierce and got a smell of it and turned around and went back to the house.

"After a little while the old man came out. He said, 'William, I am shocked and mortified beyond words. You can't realize how you have humiliated me. Here are your wages in full. Take that disgraceful machine out of my garage to-night without fail and never let me see your face again.'

"Well, that's the way it goes, just when you get a family broke in right something has to happen. I'd get another private job but it's too much worry and trouble to get them trained. I haven't got a wife on my hands any more and I can make enough for myself hacking and not so much to worry about."

THE LICENSE BUREAU

When I bought my own taxi, the Ford, I, of course, had to get it licensed. I knew the system at the License Bureau from having taken taxis there to be licensed for the boss. First I got in line with the other taxis waiting to be licensed and the first inspector would come out and look over the cars in the line and see if they were painted right and clean, etc., and he would look over your application blank. If he passed you, you went on to the next inspector, who tested your brakes. It was the proper thing to fold a two-dollar bill up with your papers; otherwise, the paint wouldn't be good enough or the car wouldn't be clean enough or something of the sort. The inspector was really quite a competent sleight-of-hand performer; you couldn't see him take the two-dollar bill but when he handed the papers back it was gone. The next inspector checked up on the brakes. He would say, "Drive down the hill fast. Now, put on the foot brake." If you stopped all right, he'd say, "Now go ahead," and when you were going fast he'd say, "Put on your emergency brake." If you stopped all right you drove into the License Bureau to have the clock tested and license plates attached, etc. The emergency brake on a Ford never was any good; wasn't built to be serviceable for over a week. The understanding was that if your emergency brake was no good you slipped the inspector half a dollar and if your foot brake was no good and you were using reverse for a foot-brake, why you slipped him a dollar. My Ford was in the latter condition. The inspector knew his business all right. I put one foot on the footbrake and put on the reverse with the other foot. He looked at me and said, "Now go ahead and try out the emergency brake." I pulled the emergency brake hard and stepped on the reverse again. He looked at me and I handed him a dollar. He said, "Now for God's sake be careful. If you run over somebody going out of the License Bureau there will be hell to pay."

The first inspector put a mark at the top of the application, which must have indicated whether you slipped him generously or not, because all the later inspectors accepted you as a long-lost friend as soon as they looked at the paper. When I got the car inside the License Bureau the fellow who tested the clock just jacked up the front wheel and spun it around a couple of times and let it down and sealed the clock. I slipped him a half. Then I went into the office to pay the license fee and get the application accepted. There was at that time a Federal Revenue tax of $10.00 a year on taxicabs and they had their collector in there, and you had to get a receipt from him before you could go through with the rest of it. He had a rule that he wouldn't accept cash. He would only accept a money order. That is, I offered him a $10.00 gold certificate in payment of the tax, which he refused to accept; I would have to go get a money order. I suppose the rule might have been put in originally so that the Post Office could check up on the inspector and keep him from stealing. "Well," I said, "what will I do? I got my car in there holding up the line."

"Well," he said, "I can get the money order for you," and he looked at me, so I got out a half a dollar and laid it down on top of the $10.00 bill and he said, "As long as you didn't know about it I will get the money order for you."

The application blank was gotten up about like the driver's license application blank, with spaces on it for two people who own their own business to vouch for your integrity, but the first inspector's check mark at the top of the application seemed to have much more influence. Well, that was the system in the old License Bureau, which was a State Bureau.

When I bought my first Packard and converted it into a taxi it was undoubtedly about the swellest taxicab in New York. I bought it from the preacher at one of those fashionable Park Avenue churches. He said one of the wealthy members of his congregation had given it to him. It was a town car with a custom-made body and the most luxurious upholstery and fittings. It cost about eight thousand five hundred dollars. After it was all fixed up and out of the paint shop and ready for the License Bureau I said to myself, "Well, now, I am going to see if I can't get this car through the License Bureau without slipping them." Packard taxis are very common now, but that car was a sensation. I took the line and when I handed the inspector my papers there was no two-dollar bill. He said that the insurance receipt among the papers was not dated right, so I had to pull out of the line to go get that attended to. Well, I just went ahead and operated the taxi the rest of that day without a license and made about thirty dollars and didn't have any trouble. The first thing again the next day I took the line. I hadn't changed the insurance receipt, but he didn't notice that this time. He said that the clock—that is, the taximeter—wasn't put on at the right angle, that I would have to have that turned around a little. So I drove out of the line and worked another day without a license. Well, the third day he said that the rug in the back of the cab was worn; I would have to get a new rug. The fourth day the outside of the car was dirty. The fifth day there was something wrong with the way the front seat was fixed. By the sixth day they must have got tired of seeing me come around because I went right on through the License Bureau without a particle of trouble, and I hadn't changed a thing.

Along about 1923 the City authorities and the Police Department had been agitating in favor of abolishing the State Bureau and putting the licensing of taxicabs in the hands of the Police Department. In 1924 the New York World staged a great expose of crookedness in the taxicab business and the police arrested a couple of inspectors of the License Bureau for accepting bribes. Great was the editorial indignation. About the only solution was to put the taxi business in the hands of the police, so the old License Bureau was abolished and the Police Department set up its own taxi licensing offices.

The first thing we were notified that we had to take out new driver's licenses and new car licenses, so I went down to the new License Bureau and got the blanks. They were just about like the old ones. The driver's license required the names of five previous employers and two business men to vouch for you and the car license, two vouchers. I got my application all filled out with the butcher and grocer I dealt with as vouchers and drove down to the License Bureau. There was quite a line of cabs waiting and I took my place on the line. The first inspector came out to look the cars over. I noticed that the first thing he did was to open the right-hand door and lift up the corner of the rug. I said to the driver next to me, "What's the game?" He said, "Put a deuce under the corner of the rug." Well, I was still feeling uppity so I thought I would try going through again without slipping them. I got past the first inspector all right and got into the License Bureau and parked the car to have the meter tested; went into the office with the application blank. The inspector said the application had to be signed by the police captain of the precinct in which I resided, so I drove out and up to the Bronx and asked the captain to sign the application. He wasn't going to sign it because he said he didn't know anything about it and had no instructions. I explained to him all over again that I was held up for his signature and I would have to have it, so he said, "Well, I guess it won't do any harm to sign it," and he did so.

I drove back down to the License Bureau, got in line again and got into the Bureau and presented the application again. The inspector said the application was made out on the wrong blank, that they had a new blank. He said, "Here, take one of these new blanks and make your application out on that." It meant that I would have to drive back to the Bronx again and get the vouchers filled out and sworn again and all that. I started filling in the part that I could fill in myself and he said, "Here, take it down to that notary public there next to the lodging house. He'll fix it up for you so you won't make any mistake." I walked down to the notary public next to the lodging house and handed him the blank. He looked it all over and turned it over and looked at the back of it, just like he had never seen one before; then he looked up at me and said, "Ah hum, I see you have to have two vouchers here." I said, "Yes." He said, "Well, I can fill this in for you and swear to it. You won't have any trouble with it. It will be three dollars and a half." I said, "Go to hell" and walked out. I went back to the License Bureau to get my car to drive back to the Bronx to get my vouchers and the Captain to sign the new application. I found that somebody had tied a red ticket on the taximeter which stated that the meter was fast and that operating the car with the ticket attached was an offense punishable by a fine of $50.00 or a year in jail. I drove out with the car and when I had gone about half a block a man ran out from a shop where they repair taximeters and called to me, "Hey, what's the matter with the meter?" I said, "The ticket says it's fast." He said, "I can fix that up for you and it won't take five minutes and you won't need to lose your place in the line or anything. It will cost four dollars and a half." I said, "Go to hell" and drove on.

I got the new application all fixed up and had the meter checked up by the manufacturers, who certified that it was all right, drove back down to the License Bureau and took the line. It was getting late in the day by that time. The cop came out of the License Bureau and called out, "No more to-day; come back to-morrow." The drivers, instead of leaving the line, all gathered around the cop. The fellows next to me said, "Well, I guess a deuce will square it," and started for the head of the line.

Well, I thought I'd try something else. I drove out of the line and went into a telephone booth and called up the City editor of The World and told him that if he was still in the humor of exposing the taxicab business I had a good story for him. He said, "Let's have it," so I told him about it. He said, "Well, it's a good story but we don't feel like using it at the present time; but you go back to the License Bureau. It's too late to attend to it now but you go back to-morrow and if you have any further trouble, call me up and I will see that you are taken care of." I thanked him and said that I would.

When I got down there the next day and was about to take the end of the line a mounted cop rode up and said, "Oh, you were here yesterday. You don't need to take the line. Drive right on in." I left the line and drove up to the door and just as I got to the door the chief of the License Bureau was standing there and he said, "Drive right on in; drive right on in. They will take care of you in just a moment." I got inside the door and there was another inspector there and he said, "Park your car right in here; park your car right in here. We will take care of you in just a moment." I went into the office and handed my application to the big chief. He ran his eye over it, smiled cordially at me and said, "Just have a seat for a moment, Mr. Hazard, and we won't detain you but a minute."

The system of licensing has been further modified so that now they have a taxi inspector in each precinct police station who attends to the licensing of all the taxis garaged in his precinct. This system is a real improvement, because some of these precinct inspectors are very decent fellows, though some of them are not.

EDUCATING THE METER

When the authorities finally decided to enforce the taxi bonding law I decided to fix the meter so it would run a little faster to make enough more to pay for the bond. There are a good many ways to make a meter run fast. The old Popp clocks were the easiest. All you had to do was to put the trunk strap around the cable tube and pull the strap tight so as to bend the tube out of line a little. The tighter you pulled the strap the faster the meter ran. The old Pittsburgh meters would jump if struck on top with a hammer. A good many of the old timers carried a hammer and a block of wood alongside of the seat. The block of wood was to put on top of the meter so the hammer wouldn't cave the case in. Most of them were very skillful with the hammer. They could strike just hard enough to make the clock register just what they thought the passenger would stand for. There were a lot of taximeter repair shops where for ten dollars you could get a clock educated, that is, fixed to run fast. The meters were all sealed by the License Bureau, but the mechanics at the shops were very good at opening up the seals and putting them back so that they looked all right.

The trouble with the educated meters was that they always ran the same and you were liable to have trouble if you picked up someone who knew how much the fare ought to be. I decided to try and fix mine so that I could let it run at the legitimate rate if desired or faster if the passenger looked right. I took the meter off and took it home and opened it up. It was a very complicated device. It cost a hundred and sixty dollars, but I wondered how they made it for less than a thousand. It took me quite a while to figure it all out. Then I made a small ratchet dog to fit onto one of the gears and drilled a very small hole through the bottom of the case at the back where it wouldn't show and ran a very fine wire through the hole and fastened it to the dog. When I pulled the wire it registered ten cents, but otherwise the meter ran just as before. It worked fine. The wire was so fine it didn't show at all and the partition in the cab prevented the passenger from seeing my hand when I reached out to pull the wire. With the wire I easily made enough more money to pay the forty-five dollars a month for the bond.

After several months the meter got out of order, as they do every so often. I kept putting off getting it repaired and used the wire altogether to make the meter work. It was quite a bother to keep track of the distance and pull the wire at the right time. Sometimes I would forget for quite a while and then would have to pull the wire three or four times in succession to catch up. A man picked me up at Chatham Square to go to Washington Heights. I started up the Bowery and what with ducking around trucks and L pillars I got a little careless about pulling the wire. The passenger said, "Hey! what's the matter with your meter? It jumps twenty or thirty cents every block or so. It will cost a fortune to go to Washington Heights at this rate."

I said, "Why, the clock has always been all right. I'll watch it and if it's fast I'll make it right with you."

I counted the blocks very carefully after that and pulled the wire at the right time. Presently the passenger said, "It seems to be working all right now. I guess I must have been mistaken. I'm sorry; I thought it was running fast, but I guess it's all right."

After the Twentieth Century Taxi Owners' Association cut the rate to twenty cents a mile the public got to riding so much that most of the passengers knew what the clock should read better than the driver. The lady says, "Your meter is fast. I made this same trip yesterday for forty-five cents." It became necessary to be very careful in sizing up the passenger.

It was a good deal of trouble to reach out and pull the wire, so I tried other ways of fixing the clock. The meter contains a unit like an ordinary clock, with a spring and balance wheel to run the meter when the car is standing and register waiting time. The speed at which it runs is regulated by the length of the hair spring on the balance wheel. I took the little wedge out that holds the hair spring and cut about an inch off of the spring and put the wedge back. The best of that is that there is nothing there to prove that the meter was tampered with. After that the meter ran at a terrible gait. You could hear it going clickety click. The waiting time registered as though you were going twenty miles an hour all the time. The only trouble was that if you got stuck in traffic on Fifth Avenue, in the Forties, say, it was liable to run up a dollar going five blocks and the passengers would let out an awful yelp.

My next device was the best of all. I found that when a certain very delicate catch failed to work the meter would register just double, that is, it would quit registering the nickels and throw a dime every time. I fastened a short length of spring wire in there so that when the flag was put straight down a projection on the shaft the flag turns on would strike the wire and push it over so it would touch the little catch and keep it from working. The wire looked as if it got left there by accident. When the flag was thrown a quarter turn the meter was legitimate, but thrown a half turn, that is, straight down, it ran double.

After that the main thing was to size up the passengers. It works like this. You get a call at Penn Station say for somewhere in East New York. You say, "How would you rather go, Bedford or Flatbush?" The fare says, "I don't know, you're supposed to know the way." So down she goes on double.

I never got into any trouble on account of over charging or having a fast clock and I never knew any one at first hand who did. I got a summons by mail once to appear before the Commissioner of Licenses to answer a complaint. When the case was called there were four people there from East New York who said that my night driver, they had his name and number, had made them pay five dollars to take them home when the meter only showed two twenty, which was the right fare. He had threatened them, they said, and so they paid what he asked. The Commissioner said, "Have you got dis driver here?"

I said, "Why, no. I didn't know what the complaint was about and I have no power to bring the driver down here, anyway."

The Commissioner said, "I tink I'll ajoin dis case till Toisday."

The four complainants looked kind of disheartened and puzzled, but they didn't make any holler and agreed to come back on Thursday.

On Thursday the driver still wasn't there. I had spoken to him about it, but he said he hadn't got a summons and wasn't going to go. The commissioner said, "Is dis driver here to-day?"

I said, "No, I told him about it, but I can't make him come."

The commissioner said, "Now if yous want to go any fuder wid dis case I'll set dis case over till next week and get dis driver in here and get dis case settled?"

The four from East New York said they didn't want to go any further with the case and so the commissioner dismissed the case and it was settled.

I had another driver who had his license taken away from him by the commissioner, but he claimed that he was innocent, that the fare who made the complaint was drunk and didn't know where he went but he had political pull. Be that as it may, it was quite a hardship for the driver, because he had to work without a license for a long time before he got a letter from the district leader and got it back.

I never could see that the License Bureau did anything but make jobs for politicians and make an opportunity for a shake down. People are funny. For instance, most any one is willing to believe that milk dealers are crooks, that they will water the milk, but they think that a milk inspector will be honest. Now why is that? They are willing to admit that they are ignorant, but they think that teachers aren't.

All the improvements that have come about in the taxi business that I know about are due to competition. Overcharging has practically passed out because at twenty cents a mile people can afford to ride so much that they are familiar with the rates. When the Twentieth Century cut the rate to twenty cents the License Bureau did everything it could to stop them. They couldn't get their cars licensed until they threatened to take the commissioner to court. Just recently some independents wanted to cut the rate to fifteen cents, and the present commissioner has successfully refused to license their cars. They took him into court, but the courts supported the commissioner, though he hasn't the slightest authority to fix a minimum rate.

In 1920 most of the cabs were old battered up cars or Fords. Then the Yellow Cab Company came into New York with new and larger and more comfortable cars. They got the business and the others had to get better cars or lose out. Then the Mogul Checkers came along with still larger and more comfortable cars and everybody followed suit. Then the rate was cut and everybody had to meet it. Then the independent driver went to buying used Packards, Pierce-Arrows and Cadillacs and converting them into taxis. This was perhaps the greatest advance in the quality of service. The cars that are built new for taxis are assembled cars. That is the manufacturer buys the motors from one concern, the bodies from another, the axles from another and so on and just patches the thing together. They are what the mechanics call junk boxes. They aren't to be mentioned in the same day with a Packard, for instance. At present you can buy a used Packard in perfect condition for five hundred dollars. With the necessary changes, the down payment on a meter and all, you can have it on the street for about six and a half or seven hundred. Now one of the assembled taxis cost about twenty-four hundred, and they cost about twice as much for gas, oil and repairs, too.

The converted Packards, etc., got the business and the taxi manufacturers had to raise their bid to the public. They started putting out town cars. One make was gotten up to look like a cross between a Packard, a German Mercedes and a Hispano-Suiza. This was a shrewd move because a town car is only used by people of great wealth. You can't use a town car unless you have a uniformed chauffeur. The back part is all nicely enclosed for the passengers, but the driver's seat is left entirely exposed. It has just the right touch of aristocratic disdain for the comfort of the driver. The twenty dollar a week clerk can take one of these town car taxis and for as little as twenty-five cents feel for the moment that he is one with Morgan and Hoover and Sinclair.

However. the independents with the converted cars have held a considerable following with the public, so the manufacturers of taxis have had a hard time to sell their cars. Now the commissioner has made a new rule that converted cars will no longer be licensed. He says that the public must be protected so he has gotten up a set of specifications for taxis and there are only two makes of taxis that meet the specifications. The Packards, Pierces and Cadillacs aren't good enough for real New Yorkers to ride in, but Paramounts and Checkers are. The commissioner also says that he will resign soon; the work is too exhausting.

If it were possible to abolish the License Bureau and make the color of a taxi a trade mark, the business would take care of itself. Time and again companies and associations of independent owner drivers have painted their cars a distinctive color and have sought the favor of the public by giving good service, but as soon as they had built up a reputation and were profiting by it others would paint their cars in imitation and proceed to ruin that reputation. A monogram doesn't work as a trade mark. It is too hard to see on a moving car. But the color is a natural trade mark. If it were made a legal trade mark some company or association would start building up a reputation for its color and the others would have to follow suit in order to live.

THE PHILOSOPHERS

I heard a group of private chauffeurs and taxi drivers and a cop, waiting at a country club, swapping opinions to pass away the time. If there had been any signs of literary or intellectual pretense about the cop's English, I would have suspected that he had borrowed his stuff from Nietzsche. The talk ran something like this:

Chauffeur (to another chauffeur): Are you still driving for ————?

Second Chauffeur: No, I fell out with them long ago.

First Chauffeur: Why, I thought you was in solid with them.

Second Chauffeur: Well, I stood in good with the old lady, but the old man was always against me.

First Chauffeur: How did you happen to leave them?

Second Chauffeur: Oh, I had trouble with the old man all the time. I got into a row with him on Fifth Avenue one day. I drove the car over to the garage and I telephoned the old lady and says, "I put the car in the garage and I'm through."

She says, "Why, what's the matter?"

I says, "I got into an argument with the boss and I lost my temper."

"Well," she says, "what did you do?"

"Well," I said. "I flew off the handle and poked him in the nose."

"Well," she says, "that's all right; maybe he'll leave you alone now. You mustn't mind a little thing like that. You bring the car around to the door to-morrow morning at nine."

Oh, I stayed on the job for several months after that. The old man was always looking for a chance to get something on me, to get me into trouble, and I don't like that.

First Chauffeur: What kind of a job have you got now?

Second Chauffeur: Oh, I got the worst job I ever had now. Of all the tightwads! He has me drive him all over the town to find a cheap place to eat. He wouldn't let me eat here. He says, "Here's a dollar; drive over to Yonkers and have supper."

He brought out three old Fedora hats; said he didn't want them any more and I could have them. You ought t'seen 'em. The grease was runnin' down from the sweat bands. I says, "No, I don't want any hats; I don't wear anybody else's hats; I can use an old suit, though."

"Well," he said, "by the time I get through with my suits they are about ready for the rag man."

He gave me an old overcoat. He must have had it made over and turned because the change pocket is on the wrong side and the inside pocket is on the wrong side. Wait a minute; I'll go and get it. You ought t'see it.

(They all examined the coat with interest.)

You know, he even cuts his own hair. I had heard about it, but I never believed it until he called me into the house to tell me something and he was in the bathroom cutting his hair. He had three mirrors rigged up around on the walls so he could see the back of his neck, and he was cutting his own hair. Can you imagine a guy with all kinds of money like that? He had an old razor strop there tied with a string. He was going to get a patent on them mirrors so everybody could cut their own hair.

The worst thing is that laugh of his. I hear him laughin' back there sometimes and I think I'll vomit. God—did you ever hear a jackass laugh?

Taxi Driver: Smith'll never get the Southern vote.

Pacifist Chauffeur: No. People from the South are afraid the Pope'll be running everything if Smith is elected, and they believe that because they don't know anything about it. It's easy to get people to believe things that they don't know anything about. I am a Catholic myself. Why, the poor old Pope hasn't got a word to say in Italy, even, outside of the Vatican, let alone running this country.

Another Chauffeur: It's all them damned favorite sons that Smith's got against him. That's what makes me sore. All them lousy little two by four favorite sons that nobody ever heard of before.

The Cop: Who's Al Smith but our favorite son?

Another Chauffeur: Aw, but Al Smith's different.

Pacifist Chauffeur: This prohibition law is making a mess out of this country. They go and pass a law like that that most of the people don't believe in; everybody violates the law and then nobody has any respect for any laws any more. Look at all these people here; they all got liquor. Then when somebody breaks a law that amounts to something, they think, "Well, what's a law?"

The Cop: Hunh, these people never did care anything about laws. You forget these are the people that make the laws.

Caretaker: You ought to see these grounds the morning after they have one of these blowouts here. Takes me a couple of days to pick up all the empty bottles and things in the shrubbery.

Second Chauffeur: Smith'll get the Southern vote all right; don't you worry. They don't give a damn about a man just so he's a Democrat. They'd vote for the devil himself, just so he's a Democrat.

First Chauffeur: Well, now, I don't know. I have always voted Democratic, but I voted for Roosevelt.

Taxi Driver: I switched once. I voted for Wilson the second time.

Second Chauffeur: Because he kept you out of war, huh?

Taxi Driver: No. My vote don't count for nothin', but with a war goin' on that way I didn't think it would be a good thing to make a change.

Pacifist Chauffeur: We oughtn't to never got in that War.

The Cop: Now you're wrong. That was the finest thing that ever happened to us.

Another Taxi Driver: I got no kick comin' against the War. I got into the shipyards and made sixteen dollars a day right along and didn't have to do no work and I got double pay on Sunday.

Pacifist Chauffeur: Well, if they have another war, they'll draft everybody and pay the munition workers and plasterers a dollar a day.

Second Chauffeur: That's what they ought to do and pay the soldiers sixteen dollars a day.

The Cop: Nah, you couldn't run a war that way. Pay a man sixteen dollars a day and you'd get some damned poor soldiers.

Pacifist Chauffeur: Well, why did we get into that War? What did we have to gain by fighting the Germans? We didn't have any more against them than against the Chinese or the Australians. We might just as well have been fighting them.

The Cop: Sure. It don't make no difference who you're fightin' just so you got a good war.

Pacifist Chauffeur: Now, I was in the Spanish American War. Think of all the men that went down there and died of disease.

The Cop: Yeah, that was no good. I was in that too. Jest sickness was all you was up against.

Pacifist Chauffeur: They died like flies in those camps.

The Cop: Yeah, and it was the big, raw-boned ones that went first. I remember a big fellow named Andrews, from the same precinct with myself, got the fever down there at Chattanooga and died.

Pacifist Chauffeur: Andrews? I remember a fellow named Andrews down there. I wonder if he was the same one.

The Cop: Oh, you couldn't tell. There was so many of 'em died. I was in the firin' squad. When you fired a salute over one o' the graves you had to be careful and not step back without lookin' behind you because they mighta dug another grave and you'd fall into it.

I remember another fellow; had a big, fat belly like that when we left. By the time we'd been down there a couple o' months he was as flat as I am. He could take his pants and wrap 'em around himself twice. He says to me, "I'm afraid I'm goin' to die. I'm afraid I'll never get home. Look at me; I ain't got no belly no more."

That was no kind of a war. I don't care who I'm fightin', whether it's Spaniards or Chinamen or Frenchmen or what. The Spaniards did the best they could, but you got to have capable people to get any action out of it. Now them Germans,—they were fine.

That Last War was something like. I wouldn't have missed that for anything. It was a little bit slow at first but after we got goin',—ah, there was action for you.

There's too many people; we got to kill off some o' these people. I been in two wars already, tryin' to kill off enough men so I'd have a chance to get married. I'm not so young any more but if we'd have a third war maybe I'd get married yet.

THE SHRIMP

I used to play the line at the night court at Jefferson Market. There was a great bunch of gorillas playing the line. There were good calls there but even with the gorillas to keep outsiders off the line there were too many cabs for the business.

There was a little guy they called the Shrimp that played the line. He was perfectly harmless, but the boys liked him and took care of him because he was always getting off wisecracks. It looked like someone would sock him for one of those wisecracks some day, but it never happened.

Dave was about the best man with his hands of the whole line. He told me all about the Shrimp. He said, "I knowed him ever since he was so high. He always was puny. We lived over on Horatio Street. Them tough mugs used to take everything away from him. He hollered so loud they picked on him just to hear him holler. He'd go hollering to his Ma and Pa. They sez, 'Fight your own battles. It will make a man of you.' They was little shrimps too. Well it was the same thing at old Public School No. 17. The teachers called him a coward. Of course they couldn't be looking after him all the time.

"He gets wise to himself though. As soon as he quits hollerin' and don't have nothin' worth takin' away they lets him alone. Well then he takes to makin' these wisecracks. The teachers calls them witty. It's funny, them cracks of his make a guy mad enough to murder him but you can't sock him. It's as much as to say he's got you right.

"When he'd finished his education he got a job as a truck driver's helper. He was at that four or five years and then he gets a chance to spell the driver at the wheel and he could drive all right so I sez to him, 'Get a Hack License.' Well he made good money hackin' right from the start."

The Shrimp didn't make much of a hit with the girls. He was shy. He took up with Sadie. She was kind of peaked and nobody went out with her, but the Shrimp had plenty of money to spend and by the time he had taken her out to parties and shows and dances for a few months she got all perked up and fixed herself up better and looked swell. She started going out with some of the big husky men and didn't have any time for the Shrimp any more.

He didn't go with anyone for a long time and then he took up with Florry. I guess he figured no one would ever take Florry away from him. She was fat and sour. He took her around and gave her a swell time. They got married and took an apartment on Ninth Avenue. He wanted to have children but Florry was afraid it would spoil her shape and she couldn't quite bring herself to face that possibility.

It got pretty tiresome for Florry sitting around the little apartment with him out hacking all night. She got to going out to the movies with a woman friend and later they went to dance halls where they paid their own admission and picked up an occasional partner.

Florry found being married no handicap in going out nights. Men hesitate to go out with a single girl because there are responsibilities and consequences to be considered, but with a married woman all of these things are already taken care of and it makes everything so much freer and easier. Even cops found Florry attractive on these terms. Often she didn't get home till six in the morning.

The Shrimp had never been in the habit of drinking. He said it went to his head too quick and got him into too much trouble. Now he started taking a shot occasionally.

One night one of the boys got the worst of it in a scrap with a hack driver over on Delancey Street so Dave went over there and found the guy and socked him. The next night when all the drivers were away except Dave and the Shrimp and another one, a gang of five came over from Delancey Street and jumped Dave and the other fellow. The Shrimp didn't join in; it wasn't expected of him. It looked like the two were going to get their lumps when somehow the Shrimp joined in. With the first crack he caught the biggest of the Delancey Street gang on the button and down he went. With that the gang ran for their cabs and beat it.

The Shrimp couldn't talk about anything else after that. He couldn't seem to get it through his head. He'd say, "One tap with that and down he goes," and he would illustrate how the man spun around and fell.

Well before long the Shrimp got into an argument with one of the boys as to who was first on the line. The other guy made a pass at him and bang the Shrimp caught him on the jaw and down he went There was no holding him after that. "See that," he'd say, "there's dynamite in that. One tap and down they go."

He came onto the line all upset one night. "I've got to quit drinking," he said. "I hit Florry." He broke down and cried. "I had to get a doctor to bring her to. She's got an eye on her like me two fists. He had to lance it or it would a busted."

Next week I heard that the Shrimp was in the hospital. The boys said he had had a drink or two and got into an argument with a cop over on Eighth Avenue. The cop made a swing at him and down went the cop. It was right near the station house and there were a lot of cops close by. They rushed him and beat him up till you wouldn't know him but he laid out two more before he went down.

Several of us rushed up to the hospital to see him. He was in the prison ward charged with felonious assault. The nurse said they had sent for his wife, that his skull was fractured and he might not live. Dave hurried out to stop her from coming. He said, "Christ! if they see that eye of hers, they'll send him up for life."

The nurse let us go in to see him. He was all over bandages and strapped to the cot. She said, "He's unconscious most of the time. We have to keep him strapped down. He came to and attacked the officer on guard here. The officer stays outside now so he can't see him."

After a bit the Shrimp opened his eyes and recognized us. He raised up and strained against the straps and said, "See them?" indicating the other patients in the ward, "them's cops. I knocked them over. Me! Me! One tap and down they go."

ALL KINDS OF PIE

This was a long time ago. The old gentleman looked like a professor or judge, small and well dressed with glasses and iron gray hair and a bristling mustache. He said, "I want you to drive me to Dun's Restaurant right up Broadway a few blocks." I pulled up at the place and opened the door. The old gentleman got out and said, "Come on in and have a bite to eat. I'll want to go farther." I said, "No, thanks. I had dinner." He said, "Well come and have a cup of coffee and a piece of pie."

It was a kind of swell place for a hack driver but I had been in court that day and had my best clothes on so I said, "All right." I look kind of like a doctor when I'm dressed up so I always fix up to go to court when I get a summons. The judges believe what I say better.

We took a table and the waiter brought the bill of fare and stood by while the old gentleman looked it over. He read off the bottom line on the bill. "All kinds of pie ten cents," and said, "Waiter, bring us one piece of every kind of pie you have and two cups of coffee." The waiter looked kind of stunned but he brought the pie on a big tray and spread the plates out all over the table. There was barely room for them. Then the old gentleman said, "Isn't that fine. All that pie for only ten cents."

The waiter said, "No, no, it's ten cents a piece."

"Yes it is," said the old gentleman peering at the bill of fare and running his finger along the line. "All kinds of pie ten cents."

The waiter said, "But you know they couldn't sell all that pie for ten cents. The boss would go broke. They don't give but one piece for ten cents anywhere."

The old gentleman said, "Hm—what you say sounds quite reasonable but still it says here, 'All kinds of pie ten cents.'"

The waiter said, "That means we have all kinds of pie. The ten cents means one piece."

"Hm—but it says, 'ALL kinds of pie ten cents,'" said the old gent.

Another waiter came over and explained it all over again. The old gentleman listened very attentively and looked quite puzzled and confused, and when the other waiter had finished he said, "I get your point and it is very well taken but it says here—'All kinds of pie ten cents.'" Both waiters started in talking at the same time and then all the other waiters gathered around and joined in. Then the head waiter shoved through the crowd and shut them up and explained it all but the old gentleman couldn't get it through his head.

Then they all talked at once again and waved their hands and shouted. I was afraid for a minute we were going to get thrown out on our ears but then I saw that they couldn't get rough with the old gentleman. He was so mild and patient and anxious to get it all clear.

Finally the proprietor came back and took a hand. He shut the others up and went at it but it didn't do any good. He gave the entire history of pie and wound up with, "So you see it is only one piece for ten cents."

The old gentleman said, "But you see it says here, 'All kinds of pie ten cents.' Now here is the pie here on the table, all kinds of pie. You see there is all kinds of pie and here is ten cents." And he laid a dime on the table.

The proprietor threw his hands up in the air and said, "I give up. Let him have it. Give him all the pie in the place. Don't charge him nothing." The waiters scattered to their tables, and our waiter made out the check for twenty cents.

When we got outside the old gentleman said, "Drive up Broadway slowly so you can stop when I tell you." In a little bit he called out, "Stop," and I pulled up to the curb. I got out and opened the door and I saw that we were in front of another restaurant. He said, "Come on in and have a bite to eat."

I said, "God I couldn't hold no more. I'm bustin' now."

He said, "Well come in and have a cup of coffee and a piece of pie." I liked to fainted, but I followed him in. Well it was the same thing all over again. We stopped at seven restaurants before he had enough pie. I thought I'd never want to look at another piece of pie.

He had me drive him home and when I got out to open the door he was leaning over reading the rate card in the back of the cab. He read, "Ten cents for each quarter mile . . ."

I said, "Hey—don't start that. Have a heart. It don't say anything about all kinds of miles."

He handed me a twenty-dollar bill and said, "There that ought to be all right. Keep the change. But it says . . ." I didn't wait to hear any more but thanked him and stepped on the gas.

THREE O'CLOCK IN THE MORNING

New York is a very unfriendly city in the day time. If you have to ride on a street car you had better get on quick or the conductor will close the door in your face and if you do make it he will try to close the door so as to catch your heels. He gives you a transfer as though you were a moral derelict to need one. If you don't ring the bell to get off but just stand by the door waiting and trusting to the motorman to see the obvious, he will go right on past your street. When you tell him you wanted to get off he'll say, "Well, why didn't you say so."

They are just as bad in the restaurants. You go into the Automat and the girls leave you standing there as though it hadn't occurred to them that you want something to eat. If you tell them what you want they go and wait on some one else just to put you in your place, and finally look at you in that condescending way as much as to say, "Did you want something?"

When you finally get your food it is best to try and find a table to yourself. If you sit down at a table with someone else it is received as an intrusion and if you are so injudicious as to say anything you are looked on as some sort of pervert with evil intentions.

But after three o'clock in the morning it is different; at least it is on Tenth Avenue. I get through work down there at anywhere from three to five o'clock in the morning. I stop in at a lunch room for a late supper or early breakfast, whichever you want to call it, and catch the owl car on its next trip north. After one o'clock they only run one car with one man on it and he makes the trip every twenty minutes.

If I don't get out of the restaurant in time to get to the corner he stops the car in the middle of the block for me. He says, "You're late to-night. Knocking 'em dead?" I say, "Oh, not so bad. How's business?" He says, "Tough. A guy with a Chrysler ran into me head on and I had to wait for the wrecker to take the car off the track." I say, "Was he hurt bad?" He says, "He was cut up pretty bad. He went through the windshield and took the steering wheel with him. They took him to the hospital. Oh, he'll be all right. A drunk can stand a lot."

If a passenger is too stewed to get on the car the conductor gets off and helps him and finds out where he wants to get off at, even when he doesn't know himself, and gets him off. One night a man got on that had been in a fight and was battered up pretty badly, and the conductor loaned him his handkerchief to wipe away the blood with.

Sam, the Greek waiter in the lunch room, knows his customers and what they like. When I come in he may say, "I saved a nice sirloin for you. If you didn't show up I was going to eat it myself." The customers are a cop or dick from the nearby station house, hack drivers, night workers in garages or factories and an occasional gunman or gorilla. They talk freely and tell each other the most intimate details of their lives.

One man is always drunk, sitting at the counter with a perfectly blank face. Sooner or later he says to Sam, "How much do I owe you?" Sam says, "Forty-five cents." The man says, "I already paid you. You are trying to put something over on me." Sam doesn't answer. After a while the man gets up and puts a dollar down on the counter and walks out. Sam says. "Here's your change." The man doesn't hear him and walks out with his face as blank as ever.

A certain hack driver shows up once in a while who tell us what big blue eyes his little boy has. Another, a big fellow, six feet tall and over two hundred pounds, makes good money playing a speakeasy in Hell's Kitchen. He makes good money because there is no competition. People hiring a cab to go to that neighborhood give the address after they are in the cab so the driver won't kick her into second and step on the gas and beat it.

They tell this story about him. Four tough guys held him up one night. All went well till they shifted their guns for an instant and pow, pow, pow, pow he stretched the four of them out with a punch a piece. I don't know if it is true or not; I never asked him; it isn't done, but if you could see him it wouldn't seem an unlikely story at all.

One night he said, "You don't talk like a New Yorker." "No," I said, "I hail from Chicago but I been all over hell." He said, "I come from Oklahoma and Texas." "How the hell did you happen to land in New York?" I said. "Oh, I had to take it on the run," he said. "I was bootlegging in a big way there. I fell out with the authorities. They wanted it all. I had to run for it. I drove the car till it fell all apart on me and my wife made the rest of the way into El Paso on foot, me carrying her. I was laid up in the hospital for two weeks having the cactus spines pulled out of my feet. I been here ever since."

One night he said, "I didn't see you here Sunday." I said, "No, I take Sunday off." He said, "What do you take Sunday off for?" I said, "Well it's this way. You see my wife works and Sunday is the only time we have a chance to be together. When I get home at night she's asleep and when I wake up in the morning she's gone."

He said, "Christ, I couldn't stand that. I been married since I was eighteen. If I was to wake up and couldn't reach out and find her hand I couldn't sleep no more. I—hell, I couldn't stand that. God, kid, you got guts."

ABSENT-MINDED

I am getting awfully absent-minded from hacking so long. The other day while I was driving I got to thinking about old times skinning a team in the San Joaquin. The next thing you know I came to myself ducking around an L pillar on Ninth Avenue and stepping on the gas to beat out a five-ton truck, and I looked back to see how mad the truck driver was, and I saw there was a passenger in the taxi.

He was quite a prosperous looking gentleman, leaning back in the cushions and smoking a cigar very contentedly.

I said to myself, "I wonder where the hell he came from. I wonder where he thinks he's going. Well, I must be going in the right direction all right or I would get a squawk out of him. I wonder where I picked him up anyway."

I drove on up Ninth Avenue and bye and bye I recollected that I had picked him up down at 25 Broadway and was supposed to be taking him up somewhere on Riverside Drive, so I got him there all right and he never knew the difference.

THE STORIES

The old man said: "Automobiles is all right and I guess they've come to stay. Horses is a back number now, but it's a pity. Now there was Old Bill.

"When I was a boy I used to go out to the country to visit my uncle Joe. He had a big farm about ten miles from town with lots of horses and cattle and hogs and everything. One day Uncle Joe said: 'Come on along, Bub, I'm going over to old man Spencer's to buy a horse. Everybody in the country has been trying to buy that horse, but the old man wouldn't let him go. I guess the old man must be pretty hard up to sell him now.'

"The farmers around there all took pride in their stock. A man might be worked to death and dirty and ragged, but he tried to keep his stock looking nice. They all knew each other's horses and cattle and would recognize a man's team on the road before they saw him.

"Old man Spencer's children had all grown up and moved away, and he and his wife kept on farming in a small way and had a pretty hard time of it.

"We drove over in the buggy and old man Spencer led the horse out. He didn't look to me like so much of a horse. He might have been a cross between a Clydesdale and a French Coach horse. He had that long head with a bulged forehead and Roman nose and long flat legs and big feet and feathers like a Clydesdale, but he was a deep-red bay, and round-barreled and smooth and neat like a Coach horse. He weighed about twelve hundred pounds.

"Old man Spencer bargained with uncle about the price, and finally uncle paid him what he asked and old man Spencer handed the halter-rope over to me. He said: 'I raised Bill from a colt.' The tears started running down the old man's face and he put one arm around Bill's neck and kissed him on the nose. As soon as he let go, Uncle Joe whipped up and we drove away quick.

"Bill certainly got plenty of work. He was good at everything. If Uncle Joe had a heavy load to haul, he always hooked Bill up with the best one of the other horses because in a pinch Bill would get down and pull like the devil himself, and then the other horse wouldn't give up as long as Bill kept on. It seemed to be a point of honor with Bill never to get stuck, and he never did. I've seen him pull the tongue out of the wagon and break a singletree, just steady pulling when the load refused to budge. The wagon might be stuck but you couldn't say Bill was stuck. I've seen him slip to his knees on an icy road but he kept right on pulling. Uncle Joe said he'd pull the hind gates off o' hell if you asked him to.

"Harry Noggins came over one fall with his mules and the corn-binder to cut corn for uncle. Harry was very proud of his mules. They were counted the best mules in the county and stood sixteen hands high. He needed three head on the binder and suggested that uncle give him two horses, so he could change them when one got tired. Uncle said he could use Bill. Harry looked insulted at uncle's idea that Bill could hold up with the mules all day.

"I went out to the corn-field in the afternoon to see the corn-binder work. Harry was hollering at the mules and throwing clods at them to keep them up with Bill, and Bill was drilling right along a little in the lead and as cool as could be. I went in and told uncle about it and he laughed and laughed and went out to see for himself. That night at supper Harry said: 'That's the biggest day's binding I ever did. What'll you take for that horse?' Uncle said: 'He ain't for sale.'

"And Bill was fast on the road too. He could take the surrey or spring wagon to town like a road-horse with a buggy, so that job fell to him too.

"It was fun taking the milk to town in the spring wagon with Bill, because he had a long easy trot that didn't look fast but ate up the miles like everything. We'd pass some one in a buggy driving a road-horse, and he'd get mad at being passed that way and whip up and pass us, but as like as not his horse would have to break into a gallop in order to do it, and that made it look worse.

"We boys used to ride him for fun and to get the cattle in. He trotted rough enough to shake all your insides out but he had a wonderful smooth canter and gallop. He liked it too. When I'd go into the barn and slip the riding-bridle on him, he'd begin to paw and toss his head. I'd mount him in his stall, and he'd back out and whirl around and come out of the barn with his head up looking for the cattle and rarin' to go.

"As soon as he located the cattle, he would stretch out and go till the wind would whistle in your ears. Usually some of the young stock would give him a run for it. As soon as he had passed them, he would bear in close, and as they turned he would turn so short that you'd go off if you hadn't slid down on the right side in advance. Then he would head them for the barn. He certainly loved to work cattle. I had to hold him in all the time, because it isn't good for dairy cattle to be run much.

"He was too smart, though. He had a way of looking around and watching you like nothing got by him. He knew how to open all the gates and barn doors. At first he was kept loose in a box stall. The door fastened with a wooden button that turned, and there was a hole in the stall door for ventilation. The rascal would stick his head through the hole and turn the button with his lips and waltz out and open the granary door that was fastened with a hasp with a padlock just hooked into it but not locked. It was too much trouble to keep it locked, because we had to get in and out frequently. We tried hooking the padlock in upside down in the hasp to fool him, but that didn't do any good. Next uncle put a halter on him and tied him to the manger with a rope, but he would untie the rope, so that didn't do any good either. We tried all kinds of knots, but he could work them all. He couldn't undo a spring snap, though, so uncle fixed all the gates and stalls with chains and spring snaps, and then we had the best of him.

"He used to play dumb about the work when he was tired, though he knew just what to do. If I'd go to hitch him up single when he was tired, he would pretend that he didn't know how to back into the shafts. He'd step first to one side and then to the other. Finally I'd whack him in the ribs and say, 'Get in there, Bill, you God-damned old fool,' and then he'd step in as nice as you please. He just sized people up and tried them out to see what he could get away with. If it didn't work, he gave in gracefully and made the best of it.

"He was good at cultivating corn. Lots of horses are always trampling the corn, particularly at the end of the row, where you have to turn around, and they get their feet over the tugs and lean against the tongue and have a terrible time, but Bill stepped around like he was walking on eggs.

"If the horses were loose in the barn lot and I opened the gate to the pasture to let the other horses out and tried to keep Bill in, he would push me right out of the way and go out unless I had a club to stop him with. I hid a club behind me once, and when he tried to push past me I hit him on the nose with it. He was mad at me then and wouldn't go into the barn. I chased him around and finally got him cornered, and he jumped the barbed-wire fence. He got his front feet over all right but came down on the top wire just above his hind feet so that the wires sagged down and left him sitting up just like a dog with his hind feet off the ground.

"I liked to died laughing at him, and he looked very much hurt. If he had struggled he would have cut himself up terribly, but he just sat there while I got the hammer and pulled all of the staples out of the fence and let the wires down to the ground and stood on them and told him to get up. He walked into the barn very slow and looked very dignified and injured.

"Sometimes uncle would unhitch Bill and let him go to the barn by himself. One time uncle stood talking to a man for a long time before following Bill to the barn. Before uncle got to the barn Bill came out. Uncle hollered: 'Bill, you get back in that barn.' Bill stopped and turned part way and looked at uncle and then looked at the gate to the corn-field. The gate was open. Don't tell me that horses can't reason. You could see as plain as day that Bill was figuring up what he stood to win or lose. He took another step toward the gate. Uncle hollered: 'Bill.' Bill stopped and turned his head around and looked at uncle, then took another step and stopped. Then he took another step and then made up his mind that it was all right and trotted off into the corn.

"Uncle just laughed and sent me to get Bill in. Bill didn't knock the corn down but just took a bite here and there as he went along. I couldn't drive him back; he was too fast for me, but after a while he turned and trotted back to the barn. He ran into his stall and acted scared to death. He pushed against his manger and pranced and looked around at me. He was just putting on, because he knew I wouldn't beat him after he had come back. I slapped him on the rump good and put the halter on and cussed him good and he seemed satisfied then. You can't beat a horse when he comes back or he'll take it that he got beaten for coming back and not for running away and he knew it.

"Bill wasn't really afraid of anything. I could drive him right up alongside of a locomotive and he wouldn't shy, but once in a while on a level stretch of road with nobody in sight he would shy at a bird flying off of a fencepost or some little thing like that. He'd throw his head and tail up and prance and snort like he was scared to death, but it always looked kind of put on to me.

"Bill never bothered the other horses much. Once in a while a new horse would come onto the place that would try to fight him, but Bill would make short work of him. Some horses like to get another horse in a corner and kick or bite him unmercifully, but Bill was too dignified for that sort of thing.

"One winter a terrible blizzard came up. It snowed and blew all day and all night, and next morning it was going harder than ever, with the thermometer at twenty below zero. Uncle Joe said the people in town needed the milk and it would have to go. He put the tongue in the spring wagon and hooked up Bill and John. He loaded up the milk, put on his big fur coat and cap and fur gauntlet-gloves and wrapped a couple of blankets around his legs and started out. The snow was drifted over the tops of the hedges. The wind was blowing so hard you could hardly stand against it, and the air was so full of snow you couldn't see over twenty feet.

"Uncle got back about noon. The snow had frozen onto his eyebrows and eyelashes. He said that he couldn't face the wind. He had to hold one glove up in front of his face and just peek out once in a while. He couldn't see the road and just left it to the horses to find the way. He said they got along fine, only a couple of times they got in so deep they got their front feet over the neck-yoke and he had to get out and clear them. The snow packed under their feet and held them up somewhat, but the wagon-wheels cut through and let the tongue down under the snow. Uncle was the only one to get to town with milk that day.

"My cousin Dick, when he was about four, liked to ride Bill when I was ploughing with Bill and John to the walking-plough. It was handy, because Dick could hang onto the hames, and if he fell off there wasn't anything to hurt him. He got so familiar with Bill that he would get right underneath of him, and if I didn't put him up on his back right when he wanted me to, he would try to climb up one of Bill's front legs. But nobody worried about it, because Bill wouldn't step on him. One time when the team was pulling, Bill's hame-strap broke and the harness slid off and carried Dick with it. Bill stopped dead and didn't move until I had picked Dick up. He was scared and crying pretty bad, and I was afraid it had spoiled his nerve for riding, so I held him until he had calmed down a little and then he wanted to get right back on Bill again. He knew it wasn't Bill's fault.

"Bill did kick me once. A hog got into the barn and ran under Bill's feet and Bill kicked at the hog and hit me. He knocked my feet right out from under me and the hog ran over me. He didn't kick any more, so I wasn't hurt much.

"One time when I was out at uncle's in the summer a terrible storm blew up. It blew and rained for three whole days, and the creek between us and town rose and flooded the bottom-lands and went over the road and the bridge, too, all except the railing. The second day of the storm my aunt got very sick. Uncle tried to telephone the doctor but the line was down. He studied it over and said: 'Bub, maybe you can get through on Bill. I'm too heavy. I'll write a letter to the doctor and you can bring the medicine back and find out what to do.'

"I put the saddle and bridle on Bill and struck out. When we got to the bottoms, Bill wanted to turn back. The bottoms are nearly a mile wide there, and the road was almost all out of sight under the water, and I couldn't remember just where it lay, but I told Bill to go ahead. He waded in slow, going very carefully. The water got deeper and deeper till it was almost over Bill's back. The road was very crooked, as it was laid out to follow the highest ground and was graded up four or five feet high. You couldn't see anything but a smooth stretch of water, with a tree sticking up here and there. Bill would turn one way and the other following the road. If he got off the road and into the barbed-wire fence, it would be all up with us, but all I could do was hold the reins and let him go. Just before we got to the bridge he had to swim a little, and then he struck the approach to the bridge and we were all right. Bill tapped with his feet on the bridge at each step to make sure before putting his feet down. The planks were all in place, so we got through.

"The doctor read the letter and said that he ought to go out, that he could get through if I could. He got his satchel and started out with his horse and buggy with me riding alongside. When we got to the water he stopped and looked doubtful. After a while I said that he could get through on Bill if he would sit quiet and let him alone, and I could wait for him in the buggy till he got back. He thought it over and said that he'd try it. He mounted Bill and I told him: 'Now let him alone. Don't try to tell him where to go.'

"Bill didn't like it at first. He kept looking back at me, but I told him it was all right, to go ahead. I could see them most of the way across and I felt sure that Bill would make it if the doctor just wouldn't get scared where the road was crooked and run Bill into the fence. Well, they made it all right, and in a couple of hours they came back. The doctor said everything was all right and he'd come out again when the water went down a bit.

"The only time Bill ever came anywhere near balking was going to church. He certainly hated to take the family to church on Sunday, particularly in the winter. There was an open shed for the horses, and I guess he got cold waiting through the long service. Sunday morning he didn't know how to get into the shafts of the surrey. Then he stopped at every gate and tried to turn off at every crossroad. He pretended to be trotting like everything, but it was all up and down and we hardly moved. Uncle didn't go to church, and my aunt held the reins and she couldn't do anything with him. Once he went lame about a quarter of a mile from the house and we thought he had picked up a nail. My aunt turned him around and he limped back home. Uncle unhitched him and picked up his feet and examined them but couldn't find anything wrong. He thought maybe he had sprained an ankle, so we hooked up another horse and went to church. The next day Bill was all right.

"When I was a young fellow, Uncle Joe sold out and moved to town, and one of the neighbors got Bill. When I was grown up I went to farming myself and I saw Bill once in a while.

"Mr. Potter, the man that owned Bill, was pretty poor, but he kept him after he was too old to work much any more. He let him run in the pasture in the summer-time and take life easy.

"Potter had a little boy and girl. They didn't have any way to get to town or any spending-money, so one June they picked a lot of cherries and got Old Bill up from the pasture and rigged him up with some old bits of harness patched together with string and wire and hooked him up to an old tumble-down spring wagon. They drove to town to peddle the cherries and get some spending-money. The little girl would stay in the wagon and mind the outfit while the boy went around to the back doors to sell the cherries.

"Once while the boy was in one of the houses making a sale, the old bridle fell apart and came off, and Old Bill, seeing himself free, took a notion to start out for home. The little girl sawed on the lines, but of course it didn't do any good with the bit under Old Bill's neck. A lot of women sitting out on the front porches got scared and ran out and screamed till a man stopped Old Bill. Then the boy came out from the house and they all gave him hark from the tomb for leaving his sister in the wagon; said she might have been killed and so on.

"I was on my way to town and arrived on the scene just at this time. I spoke up and said: 'Now hold on, folks. I've known this horse all my life and he wouldn't run away and hurt anybody. I used to read the paper all the way out to the farm driving him with the lines hooked over the dashboard. If all you people had as much sense as Old Bill here has, you'd have something to be proud of.' So they shut up and let the boy alone.

"Mr. Potter wouldn't let them peddle fruit any more on account of the accident. He said it would look as though he wasn't taking proper care of his children. But Old Bill got a job peddling again before long.

"A Mr. Morris in town had gone broke in the coal business and went insane. Not very bad but he couldn't work. His wife ran a little store and the six kids helped in the store and carried papers and did anything they could to bring in a little money, and so they got along. They borrowed Old Bill after the Potter children had to quit and went to peddling vegetables that they bought at wholesale. They made out fine at it. They were very likable youngsters and I imagine that people bought more from them than they could use. They got out and pushed the wagon to help Bill up the hills. Old Bill of course played dumb with them, and they scolded him and slapped him with the lines, and altogether they all had the time of their lives.

"Well, there were a lot of old women in the town that had outlived their usefulness and they got the idea of organizing a society for the prevention of cruelty to animals. The opposition women that got left out of that society started one of their own for the prevention of cruelty to children. The first outfit came down on the Morris children for abusing Old Bill and had them up in court. The second gang hadn't had a case yet, so they came down on Mr. and Mrs. Morris for not providing for the children. It looked for a while like the kids were going to be sent to a home and Old Bill was going to be shot. Some neighbors offered to put up enough money to keep the Morrises going and keep the family together. The children didn't want to accept charity when they could take care of themselves, but they decided it was better than going to jail. Potter came in and claimed Old Bill, and so there he was back in the pasture again.

"One spring I needed an extra horse to take the milk to town so the others could keep on ploughing. I couldn't find a cheap horse in the country, but Mr. Potter said I could have Old Bill if I would take good care of him.

"Bill was about twenty-four years old by that time and hadn't done any work for quite a while. His teeth were all worn down to little round knobs at the roots, so he couldn't chew his feed good, and he was thin, hadn't shed yet, and looked terrible. But for all that, he was absolutely sound in wind and limb.

"I took him and started feeding him fresh-cut alfalfa uncured and crushed oats, and he ate it fine. The second day I decided to see if he could make the trip to town. As soon as I started putting the harness on, he threw his head up and started stepping around. He started down the road with his head up and his tail over the dashboard, but in about a mile the sweat was running down his legs, and though he was trotting fast, the wagon was hardly moving. I stopped him and let him rest till he was ready to go again. We finally got to town and back again, but poor Old Bill was white with lather and about all in, but you could see he was proud of himself.

"The feed agreed with him fine and he put on some flesh and shed off nice, and his new coat shone in the sun. He did much better as time went on, but he would still trot straight up and down in one place when he got tired instead of stopping before he was told to. There was one bad hill to climb and he'd take a good rest before he tackled it. Then he'd dig in and go up it like he used to when he was a four-year-old, but he had to be rested again at the top.

"One day we met two strangers on the road in a buggy. They stopped and motioned me to stop. One, an old man, got out and came over and said: 'I'm a veterinarian, just moved to town, and I'd like to get your work. Now, your mare here is kind of poor. You bring her in to me and I'll fix her up so she'll feed better and put on flesh.'

"I said: 'He's a horse. He's twenty-four years old.'

"He said: 'I know her teeth are bad. I'll file them down so she can chew her feed.'

"I said: 'He ain't got any teeth.'

"The other man got out and said, 'He's terrible deaf,' and then he hollered in the vet's ear: 'It's a horse, twenty-four years old.'

"The old vet. said: 'Never mind. I know she's got the bots. I can get rid of them and she'll put on flesh.'

"Me and the other fellow shouted together: 'He's a horse. He's a horse.'

"The old fellow said: 'I know she's horsin'. You can't tell me nothing. I been a veterinarian for fifty years.'

"We all shouted together and then the other fellow shouted in the old man's ear till he understood. He looked kind of crestfallen, and then he climbed back in the buggy and they drove off.

"After the spring work was over I didn't need Old Bill any more, so I kept him out in the pasture. There was a missionary preacher who used to come out to my place with his wife and three children to tramp around the pasture, and they took a liking to Old Bill. The children rode him and brought him sugar and carrots.

"When they found out that I didn't need him they wanted to take him home with them for the children to play with. They had a little one-acre place just out of town. I never had much use for preachers and missionaries in particular, but this fellow wasn't so bad. It was a lot of trouble to get out and cut a bushel of fresh alfalfa for Old Bill every morning. I told the preacher all about how Old Bill had to be fed, and he promised to treat him right, so I let him have him. They led him off down the road with the children dancing around him.

"I went over to see how Old Bill was getting along in a week or so. They had a tight little barn, and Old Bill was lying down in his stall asleep. He was bedded down about a foot deep with straw, and the children had spread an old blanket over him and put two pillows under his head."

I was delayed getting back to the farm and had to stop at a strange farmhouse and ask if they could put me up for the night. They made me welcome and had a couple of vacant stalls in their horse-barn for my team.

They were rather poor, shiftless farmers. There were a lot of children. The mother looked overworked, and the man looked worried and worn out. His horses were poor stock and in bad condition. There was a whole pack of thin, hungry dogs running about the place. I wondered why he didn't kill them off. Why let them live and starve? He looked rather wistfully at my team. Jerry and Betty were French coach stock, dark bay, well built and well kept, and intelligent. I worked my horses hard and fed them well; they had all they could clean up, of the best. I never asked them to do more than they could, and they never failed me.

It was with relief that I took the road the next morning. Some miles down the road I discovered that two of the dogs had followed along under the wagon. They looked like pretty well-bred collies, but they were only about half-size though mature, thin and shaggy and wolflike. I tried to drive them back, but they circled around and stayed with me. Finally I gave it up and when I got home they were still under the wagon. They slunk off into the corn-field and I didn't see anything more of them that night. I put up the team and fed them.

When I went down to feed the team the next morning I found the two dogs in the horse-barn lying in the hay in front of Jerry's and Betty's mangers. They slunk out of the barn as soon as they saw me, while the horses tossed their heads and went "hunh, hunh, hunh" in expectation of breakfast. After breakfast I called the dogs from the house to give them something to eat, but they didn't show up, so I took a pan of scraps down to the horse-barn for them. They wouldn't come up to eat, but as soon as I got ten feet away they went at it and wolfed it down. I tried to make friends with them, but it couldn't be done. They wouldn't eat until I got a certain distance away, and they never thanked me.

They always slept in front of Jerry's and Betty's mangers, and wherever Jerry and Betty went, they went. I named them Bill and Jack. Bill usually ran behind the team and Jack ran in front of the team. If I was ploughing, they would follow the team out to the field, and after I had made one round they would lie down under the hedge at the corner of the land and watch us go around and around, and when we knocked off and went to the house, they followed. When I had hauling to do on the road they followed the team, no matter where I went.

They got into lots of fights with other dogs along the road. They always trotted along very meekly and looked an easy mark for the other dogs. Jack, being in the lead, would be attacked first. He never seemed to see the attack coming—kept on going straight ahead—until they were right on him and then he struck and surprised them. If they were big dogs, or if there were several of them and Jack didn't drive them off immediately, Bill would slip around from behind about the time all their attention was concentrated on Jack and attack from the rear whatever dog Jack was facing. That manœuvre always broke the spirit of the enemy.

I remember one place where a huge mastiff, pretty near as big as a small Shetland pony, came leaping over the hedge, followed by half a dozen lesser dogs, to attack Jack. He didn't appear to notice them as the mastiff bore down upon him, and the mastiff hesitated just a little bit before striking, and Jack had him by the throat. He had waited until the enemy's teeth seemed to be within an inch of him before he showed any recognition of their presence. The mastiff thrashed him around, trying to throw him off his feet and break his hold, and the other dogs edged in on Jack. My heart was in my mouth watching him. One got within a couple of inches of his haunch before he let go of the mastiff and whirled and struck him and whirled back and struck the mastiff again. Then the other dogs closed in and it looked like it was all up with poor Jack, when Bill took the mastiff from the rear. As he yelped and half turned Jack slashed his throat. He headed back over the hedge, with his tail between his legs and his head down, about four times as fast as he came out, and the rest of the pack followed him.

They never attacked other dogs, but for all of that there was a continual commotion when we were on the road. I was afraid of getting into serious trouble with the neighbors over them, but it was such a circus to watch them and there wasn't any way to keep them from following the team, so I let it go.

I got a hired hand who had an intense affection for animals, and he tried every way he could think of to make friends with those dogs. If he could get them in a corner he could pet them, and the dogs wouldn't bite, but they wouldn't wag their tails nor look pleased, and they would slink off as quickly as they could. I would have liked to have had friendly dogs around the place that I could have used when driving the cattle, but as long as I had Bill and Jack there was no use to get any other dogs, and so we went on for some two or three years.

Then Sally said that something was making off with eggs and chickens. I watched and finally caught Jack coming out of the hen-house with an egg. He snarled and ran for the horse-barn. I went into the house and got the pistol. There is no use in monkeying around with a dog that gets after the eggs and chickens. I have never seen any one have any success in breaking them of it. I walked down to the horse-barn, and as I approached the door Jack ran out and into the edge of the corn and stood half turned watching me. I held the pistol up and shook it and said: "Jack, next time I'll kill you." I didn't quite have the heart not to give him one chance.

Everything seemed to be all right for a couple of months, and then one morning I saw Jack running out of the chicken-house with a hen. He dropped the carcass and ran for the horse-barn again. I went in and got the pistol and walked down to the horse-barn and, as before, Jack ran out as I approached and made for the corn. Just as I was ready to fire Bill came out of the barn door straight at me. I fired and swung the muzzle of the pistol just in time to plug Bill. The force of the bullet stopped him in midair as he leaped, and he dropped at my feet. I had got him right between the eyes and he only quivered a little. I had got Jack just back of the shoulder and he only went a couple of jumps from where he was struck.

I went up to the tool-house and got the spade and buried them behind the horse-barn.

AND THE COPS GOT THEIR MEN—
INCLUDING THE TAXI DRIVER

Yes, I seen the finish of the chase. Business was dull, even a little worse than usual. My supply of home brew was running low so I drove up to the malt and hop store and bought supplies and went home and started a new batch. Then I started out to hack again. I was just turning from Seaman Avenue into Dyckman when I heard a motor back-firing. I looked up and seen a cream-colored taxi, a Monarch cab, coming out of Riverside Drive. The driver was hunched over the wheel with just the top of his head showing. He was bare-headed and had curly red hair. There was a man in a reddish-brown suit on the back seat of the cab sitting tight in the right-hand corner. Twenty feet behind them was another cream-colored taxicab, a Checker, with the driver sitting up straight and a cop standing on the running board with a pistol in his hand. The first cab had two big holes in the back window. The cop raised his pistol and fired twice. I understand that bullets come out of pistols that may kill people but it seemed unlikely. I couldn't see the bullets and didn't see any effect from them. The first cab was only going about twenty-five miles an hour but it didn't slacken speed, the driver was still crouched over the wheel and the man in the back sitting tight.

I thought they must be trying to escape after a robbery. They must have picked an old worn-out cab or else something had gone wrong with it or they would go faster. The man at the wheel looked like he was nursing it along the best he could. His curly red head didn't move. Back of the second cab the Drive was full of cars running on both sides of the road with men on the running boards with pistols in their hands. For all the bandits were going so slow the pursuers weren't gaining on them. I thought, "I could step on it and pass them easy and cut in in front and force them to the curb. But then why should I? Two against New York. And what chance have they with the old boiler gone back on them and hundreds after them with the city behind them and glory to win?" But the curly red head stayed crouched over the wheel, a nursing the old bus along. Maybe they'd been hungry and desperate, thought it better to take a big chance than die by degrees of dull misery.

I'd been held up and robbed myself and I didn't like it. I'd always figured that if I ever got the chance I'd do my bit to pay off that score against the holdup guys. That's the trouble with them guys. They go and pick on people that are maybe no better off than themselves. Why don't they knock off some of their real enemies? The cops are decent enough men, doing their day's work to make a living. But then they take their orders from the big crooks.

I turned and followed the bandits just like the rest of them, at a reasonably safe distance. They crossed Broadway without slackening right in front of the traffic cop on duty there. He stepped in front of them and held up his hand for them to stop and then stepped back to keep from getting run over, completely confused by this brazen affront to the New York Police Force. When the bandit's car was twenty feet past him he caught on and whipped out his gun and fired twice at them but it didn't seem to do no good. Then he jumped on the running board of the car ahead of me.

I could have shot right around the whole mob of cars with my eight-cylinder Packard but I didn't want to get in front of any of the shooting and behind it there was the damndest mess of cars jockeying around and cutting each other off that I ever saw. They'd all gone crazy, everybody trying to get ahead of everybody else and still not get too close to the shooting. I know I used the brake more than the throttle. There was a burst of pistol shots every little while and scattered shots in between but the guy with the curly red hair just kept on nursing her along.

I wondered if the driver was one of the gang or just the taxi driver the bandits happened to pick. When I get a call and the passengers treat me like a human being I do the best I can for them. Maybe he was like that and when he found out how bad it was he thought "I'm in now and I may as well go through." And then when he saw it was hopeless, said, "Well, I ain't going to back out now." At any rate he was nursing that old can along the best he could.

At Nagle Avenue he turned South with the hounds and the sightseers close behind but not too close. It sounded like the Fourth of July. But they dragged along so slow. Why the hell didn't they get one of those new Fords, something that could knock off seventy or eighty miles an hour? At Broadway he turned North again and a cop fell from the running board of a taxi and his driver slumped down in his seat and came to a stop. At Sherman the bandit turned off again, still not making more than thirty miles an hour. At Dyckman the driver seemed to hesitate and then turned East again. The cars in front of me came to a stop and I was blocked. I left the car in the middle of the street and ran around the corner. There was the bandit's car stopped behind a truck that blocked the road. The cops and dicks were running up to it. There was a steady rattle of shots. When I reached the cab it was over. The driver was lying with his head and shoulders hanging out the righthand door face down with his hands stretched out limp in front of him. His curly red head was still untouched but blood was pouring out of him underneath onto the asphalt. I never thought there was that much blood in a man. His socks had come down and his low shoes were worn at the heel. His bare shanks looked kind of scrawny. He didn't have any coat on and his shirt tail was coming out. His pants were that cheap cotton stuff like you get in an eight-dollar suit. The man in the reddish-brown suit was hanging out of the right rear door in the same way only face up. His face and hair and hands were drenched with blood. The cops were dragging a third man I hadn't seen before from the floor of the cab and putting him in another taxi. There was hardly any blood in the cab, it was all on the asphalt so they must have been killed just as they were trying to get out.

I stood there and wondered why death is so affecting. The bandits were certainly no worse off than plenty of other people in New York. Only a few years ago about a hundred thousand of our young men got the same thing in a scrap they didn't know any more about than I know about this one, and lots of nice things were said about that.

The cops were completely addled. They milled around the cab and didn't seem to know what to do. One said, "They got two cops." Another said, "No, they got three. Yeah, they got Churchill." One picked up a couple of thirty-eight caliber automatics from the bottom of the cab and said, "I guess I better turn these in." He looked at them for a while and squinted down the barrels and then laid them down on the running board of a car that was parked at the curb there, and stepped over one of the bodies and picked up a handful of empty shells from the floor of the cab and looked at them and laid them down on the running board. One said, "We'd better search this cab," and leaned in and pulled out the driver's hack license card from its rack and looked at it and handed it to another cop and he looked at it and handed it on. Then they scooped up a double handful of empty cartridge shells apiece from the back of the cab and stood around and didn't know what to do with them and finally all laid them down again on the running board.

One picked up a fat canvas money bag, such as the banks use, all nice and clean and still tied tight around the top with a string. He looked at it vacantly and set it down on the fender of the parked car right under my nose. The cops picked it up and stared at it one after another and put it down again. I thought, "I wonder if any one would notice if I picked that up and walked off with it. There's probably enough there to buy a small farm and stock it so I could live in peace and comfort the rest of my life."

HACKING NEW YORK
Scribner's Nov–Dec 1929

These are the real experiences of a New York taxi-driver,
and in effect they present New York of to-day in a series
of graphic short stories.

I.

CAME TO NEW YORK

I came to New York just to see the sights, particularly Greenwich
Village, and I made some friends in the Village. About that time
my money ran low, and I thought I had better get something to
do to live on. Hack-driving seemed to be a very handy way to see
New York and eat at the same time, so I talked to hack-drivers
about the business of getting a license. Following their
instructions I first got a chauffeur's license from the State. Then I
went over to the taxi-license bureau and got an application.

In the application I was supposed to put down the names of
my employers for the past five years. My employers for the
previous five years were scattered all over the United States and I
had forgotten how many there were, so I got out a newspaper and
turned to the legal notices and picked, out the names of five
bankrupt firms.

I had to declare whether I had ever been in jail or not and, if
so, when, where, and how. I had been in jail once out in California
along with another fellow, but we had slipped the jailer two
dollars and he had locked us in a cell previously occupied by some
yeggs who had dynamited a hole in the floor and dug a tunnel out
along the sewer-pipes, so we got out and caught the next train. As
this left no record, I felt no uneasiness in answering the question
with a "no."

The application required me to have two men in New York
who owned their own business make out vouchers for me stating
they had known me so long and I was thoroughly honest and
reliable, etc., and swear to them before a notary public. I went into
the delicatessen-store and bought about a dollar's worth of
provisions and got the delicatessen dealer to make one out
without having it sworn. I went into the cigar-store next door,

bought a carton of Camels, and got him to fill out the other one. Then I had to get my last previous employer sign another voucher for me, swearing that I was of unblemished character and that he was eager to hire me again. I had one of the Greenwich Villagers swear he had employed me as chauffeur. Then I went back to the license bureau, and there are a lot of notary publics located around there who will let you swear to anything for a quarter apiece. As I remember it, there was a dollar's worth of swearing to be done.

Next the hack-drivers told me I would have to stand an examination as to knowledge of the city—all the piers, hotels, out-of-the-way streets, etc. I would have to be finger-printed and would have to leave photographs of myself, which would be investigated by the police department for ten days to see if I had any police record. But they also informed me that by slipping a certain man in the office ten dollars I could avoid all these formalities and get a license right away. They told me how to pick him out. I went in and spotted him all right, called him over to one side, introduced myself, and shook hands with him, with a ten in my palm. He said: "Have they got anything on you?"

I said: "Nope."

"Come back at two o'clock."

I went back at two o'clock, and he had the book and badge and everything all ready for me.

About five years later when I was in there I heard them examining some applicants as to their knowledge of the city. They asked them the location of some places I don't know yet.

BREAKING INTO THE TAXI GAME

When I got my license I already had a job in sight. I went to work the same day for a fellow who had one cab. He drove it himself in the daytime and hired me as night driver. He had a stand-in with the private cops at Grand Central and told me how to work it there, so I made my start in the height of the rush hour at Grand Central. Luckily my first call was to Penn Station, and I knew where that was anyway, but I didn't know where cars were supposed to drive in, so I set him off on Eighth Avenue. Apparently he didn't know any better either, and I got just as good a tip as one might expect.

The next call was down-town somewhere. I hadn't a notion where it was, so I started off in the direction I was headed, and after going a block and a half I turned and said: "Well, now, where is that place anyway?" They didn't want to get out after having gone that far, so they told me how to get there and I made out all right. I worked that scheme right along and didn't have any trouble, though I got into some terrible mix-ups making theatre calls—I did get some awful bawlings out from the cops in the theatre district—in fact, I made more in a way than I made after I knew the city. I got a call to Coney Island and rambled all over Brooklyn, ran up about twelve dollars on the clock, and got it with a substantial tip without a whimper. I never would have had the nerve to pull anything as rough as that if I had known how to get there. I never have got as much since for a trip to Coney Island.

TRAFFIC

At first I was always violating traffic regulations. I tried telling the cops that I was new at the business as an excuse for getting tangled up, but I found that didn't do any good at all. They said: "Aw, that's what they all say."

During the first two or three months I got about all the different kinds of summonses there are. However, I became pretty good at talking them out of it. If a taxi-driver tells a cop that he didn't know about it or it wasn't his fault, he is sunk; he'll get a ticket sure. But if you admit that you pulled a boner or that you didn't think he was looking or something of that sort, they are very apt to let you off, because they know that we make our living on the streets day and night in all weather just the same as they do.

I got caught passing a street-car on the wrong side on East Broadway and got a summons for the eight-foot law, which carries a minimum fine of twenty dollars. The cop says: "What's the matter? You ought to know better than that."

I said: "Well, we have been passing those cars on the wrong side right along; it's the only way to get by them; and I didn't know they had a cop here."

When I appeared in traffic court the cop had about a dozen truck-drivers that he had given summonses to for not keeping close enough to the curb. This violation carries a small fine. He lined me right up with the truck-drivers, and the clerk of the court read off the one charge for the whole outfit, then went through the papers and said to every one, "How do you plead?" and we all said, "Guilty, guilty, guilty," down the line. The judge said, "Two dollars apiece," so we filed past the cashier and handed in our two bucks.

There is an ordinance that taxis are not allowed to stand except at designated hack-stands. This ordinance is enforced only on special occasions in case the property-owners complain or there is some particular reason. I used to stand down in front of the Customs House, which is forbidden territory, and got good business there in the daytime. The cops would merely chase me out once in a while. One day the cop came along with a man in plain clothes. He told the cop to give me a summons for standing there. The cop stalled around and said he thought I hadn't been there very long and asked me what I was standing there for. I told him I had had a call down there and had stopped to light a cigarette. The cop was going to let me off but the other fellow insisted on his giving me a summons.

When we get up in traffic court the cop said: "Say anything you want when you get up there. I tore up your record." (The courts keep a full record of every taxicab chauffeur's summonses and the disposition made of them, and it is supposed to be laid before the judge along with each new summons.) I told the judge the same story I had told the cop. The cop said I had been there only a minute or two. So the judge let me off with a dollar fine.

Some hack-drivers have a terrible grouch against cops, but they are usually the kind of men who never could be in the wrong; such a thing just couldn't happen. I have run into some pretty low skunks among the cops, but take them all in all, I think they are a very decent body of men.

The traffic-court magistrates are very rough on taxi-drivers, but I think, after all, they have to be. It certainly is true that a taxi-driver isn't in a position to plead ignorance.

I was up in the traffic court for a second-offense speeding, the fine for which is fifty dollars, which I could ill afford to pay. I thought of trying to talk them out of it, but watching the cases ahead of me, it seemed as though the ones who talked got charged for it. One fellow told about how he had eight children to support and couldn't spare the money. The judge said: "I will take all that into consideration in your case and make it as easy as I can for you. Fifty dollars or ten days." I thought I might just as well keep my mouth shut. The cop said if I wanted to plead guilty and pay the fine, I could go before another judge and get it over quick, so I joined the procession through the judge's private rooms.

The clerk at the door kept mumbling: "How do you plead?"

The defendants, "Guilty, guilty, guilty," as they went by.

The judge: "Fifty dollars apiece."

The cashier took in the money and gave receipts.

Well, after all, I knew I was speeding and was figuring on not getting caught. And I expect the man with the eight children knew he was speeding, too, and he probably knew he had the eight children; that is, if he did actually have them.

GRAND CENTRAL

I found a summons in the mail one morning to appear before the commissioner of licenses on the complaint of the New York Central. I didn't know just what it was all about. There had been about half a dozen of us who had been slipping the special cop at the entrance on Vanderbilt Avenue fifty cents a night to look the other way and give us a chance to pick up calls there. That entrance is intended for private cars and independent taxicabs to discharge passengers. In spite of the fact that the company cabs have a private entrance down on the level where the trains come in, where they have starters and signs and everything to direct the people where to get the cabs, a lot of passengers come up to that Vanderbilt Avenue entrance, so there is good business there, and they are usually good calls. On that account the company has to put a special cop there to chase the taxicabs out, because cabs discharging passengers will linger as long as possible in the hope of picking up one, thus preventing other cars from coming in. Our understanding with the cop was that we were to linger only so long, and if we didn't get anything, we were to cruise around the block, then dodge in again. We all knew when the trains were breaking and how to manage it.

The cop got hungry and let a whole lot more in on the racket, and there got to be so many of us, there was scarcely enough business for us and everybody was inclined to stall longer.

I went down to the license bureau at the time specified in the summons. There was a whole crowd of hackmen who worked around Grand Central.

The commissioner called us all into his office, closed and locked the door. "Now," he said, "you are all old-timers and I can speak frankly. I know the situation there at Grand Central. We tried to have the Vanderbilt Avenue entrance declared a public hack-stand and protect your rights there. We even went to court with it, but the Railroad Company owns the property, and we lost. Now, you've got me into a jam. The president of the New York Central tried to drive in there in his limousine Monday, and there were so damned many taxicabs in there stalling that he couldn't get in and had to get out in the middle of the street and walk in. There has been a lot of pressure put on me to make an example of you fellows, but I'm not going to do it. I brought you up here to serve notice on you that if any of you fellows get caught stalling in there again, I'll break you. And don't come up here with any letter from any politician or with any hard-luck story. This is fair warning."

TWO WOMEN AND BENNY LEONARD

I had a call to Grand Central. As I let the party out, I knew there was a train breaking right then. The cop was after us, chasing the empty cabs out. I stalled, putting the money in my pocket, closing the cab door, putting the flag up, and still the people weren't coming out from the train. Just then a cab cut in in front of me so that held me for a while. The cop tried to make me back up and get out, and while I was monkeying around, I managed to stall the motor, so I had to get out and crank it. The cop was frothing at the mouth. By the time I got back on the cab, two middle-aged women came out and wanted a taxi, so I opened the door for them, and the cop was fit to be tied. They got in. They wanted to tell me right there all about where they were going, but I told them I would drive outside and they could tell me then.

I got out and pulled up at the curb and they gave me an address away up in the Bronx. They said they were going to visit their niece who was teaching school in New York. I knew from their accent they came from the Middle West the same as I did. They might have been my own aunts. Well, when I got them clear up in the Bronx, I found there wasn't any such number. It was away after dark; business places were closed. I tried to hunt up the woman's name in the telephone-book. It wasn't there. I tried looking for the same number on streets that had similar names; couldn't find it. Finally I called up the Board of Education; I didn't expect to find anybody there, but I did, and they hunted up this woman's address from their records, so I drove to that address. The landlady said she had moved, but she had her address. I took that address, chased it down, and, by golly, it was right; she was really there. Well, the two women were too pleased and grateful for anything, and one of them said: "And it's only four fifty. Isn't that reasonable." She handed me five dollars and they both thanked me. Well, sir, I just simply didn't have the heart to break the sad news to them that it was fourteen fifty on the clock. I took the five-spot and thanked them, drove off, and kicked myself all the way downtown. I says to myself: "I'll certainly have to go like hell to-night to make up that ten bucks for the boss."

I ran along and ran along, picking up short calls, and figuring I would have to turn in an I. O. U. Finally I made the break at the fight at the Garden, and I picked up Benny Leonard and four other pugs. I took them up to 114th Street and Seventh Avenue. There was two forty on the clock. Benny says, "How much is it?" and I says: "Three eighty." Benny hands me four bills. Three of them were ones and one was a ten. I thanked him but started in second.

THE FORD AND CHATHAM SQUARE

I bought a Ford taxi painted brown and white and made much better money for a time cruising for business at the then low rate of thirty cents a mile than I had made before bucking the lines, but as time went on more and more cabs were painted brown and white, a lot of the cab-stands were abandoned, and there got to be more cabs cruising than there was business, so I tried playing some of the old deserted stands again.

I picked out one on Seventh Avenue and did pretty well there, but the others who saw me standing there took to playing the stand too, so pretty soon there were eight or ten cabs on the stand. Then some of the old-time buckers came back on the stand with high-rate clocks. They claimed that the stand was an old buckers' stand and it rightly belonged to them. One by one they managed to chase the low-rate men off the stand, and finally I was the only one left. As long as I played the stand, I naturally got the preference with a low-rate clock, and the buckers, of course, didn't like that, so I finally decided I couldn't hold the thing down all by myself.

I went to another one of the old-time abandoned stands. The same thing happened there.

Finally I tried standing at Chatham Square at the corner of Mott Street, which is Chinatown. I did well there for quite a while, as the drivers of low-rate cabs weren't so quick to line up behind me on the stand because the neighborhood has a very bad reputation.

I found the Chinese to be very good customers. I didn't overcharge them, and they appreciated the fact and gave me lots of good business.

It was quite an interesting location. There is supposed to be a cop on post there all the time, and the cops and plain-clothes men were passing all the time. In spite of this fact, a couple of pickpockets used to hang out on the corner there in front of the cigar-store. I got quite well acquainted with them. They didn't seem to be at all reticent about the business. The little thin one who did the real work showed up in a nice new suit one day and I spoke about it. He said: "Yes, I have been needing a suit for a long time, but business has been terrible. You have no idea. I ordered this suit made quite a while ago, paid a deposit on it, but couldn't get it out. I promised the tailor to get it out yesterday. I got up in the morning and I just had car-fare. Well, coming down on the car I got a guy for sixteen dollars. The conny (conductor) was one of these fifty-fifty guys. I told him I only got six and gave him three. I should give him eight! What did he do to earn it? That give me thirteen, and I owed thirty-five on the suit. Well, I changed to another car and got another guy for ten. By the time I got down here I had enough to get the suit out, and now I'm broke again."

I says: "How is it about getting caught? Have much trouble that way?"

"Oh," he says, "it's bad now. It ain't what it used to be. It used to be that if you got a stretch the warden would let you out if he knew you, and all you had to do was to show up when he needed you, when the inspectors were around or something like that, and turn him in a bit every day. But that's no good any more. A lot of crooks got into the game and didn't show up when he told them to and got him into a jam. You can't blame him; he's got to protect himself."

VAIT FOR HIM

I was playing the Chatham line one Tuesday night when business was dull. The drivers all gathered up around one of the cabs and got to talking. One said he had a good waiting call. Another said: "Waiting call. You don't know anything about good waiting calls. Listen to this one. Remember last Wednesday it was raining? I was on day shift and I picks this guy up in the mornin', big, swell-lookin' guy, and he keeps me the whole day, just short runs and waitin'. Along in the afternoon he goes into a swell apartment-house. Well, I waited an hour and I commenced to get worried, so I goes in and asks the elevatorman if he knows this guy. He says: 'Sure, he's all right. His name's Klein; he's here right along.' So I goes back and sits in the cab; smokin' cigarettes; and the rain drizzlin' down steady, and I waits another hour. Then I goes in and asks the telephone-operator to call this guy up and ask him if he wants the cab to wait any longer. He says: 'Tell him to wait; I want him to wait.'

"Well, half past four come and I was supposed to be in the garage by four, but I didn't know what to do, so I called up the boss and told him about it and asked him what to do. The boss is a Jew. He says: 'You ah gattING a dollAH end a hef an ouAH end die cah is stendING? VAIT for him! VAIT for him! If it is rainING go inSIDE; get a cup COFFee but VAIT for him! VAIT for him! Get in die bek of die ceb; mek yourself comfortable but VAIT for him! VAIT for him!'

"I got in the cab and waited and waited. Six o'clock come and seven o'clock, and the meter was clicking right along. I got out and wound it up once in a while. Nine o'clock come and there was thirty-five dollars on the clock, and I gets worried again, so I had the telephone-operator call him up again. He says: 'You tell him I want him to wait for me; if he's scared of his money, I'll pay him now. But I want him to wait for me.'

"I told the doorman I'd pay for the coffee and sandwiches for the bunch if he would go and get 'em, so I minded the door and he went and got lunch for us. Then I crawled back in the cab and took a nap for a while. I was scared to call him up any more for fear he'd get sore.

"He never came out until seven o'clock the next mornin'. He was lookin' terrible. He had a girl with him. 'Now,' he says, 'I want you to drive me over to Tiffany's because I want to buy my sweetie some jewelry.' Well, we drives down Fifth Avenue and stops in front of Tiffany's, and they ain't open yet, so we waits there, and the cop was givin' us the eye. He looked terrible. Finally they opened the store and they starts to go in and the doorman won't let 'em in. Oh, he looked terrible. He pulls out the roll and the doorman lets him in then. Then the clerks wasn't goin' to wait on him, until he gets the roll out, and then he got service.

"After that he drops the girl off at the apartment-house and I takes him up to New Rochelle. What a call!

"Well, that wasn't all there was to it. You see, this guy was one of the big men in the Mongoose Taxi Manufacturing Company, and the boss said that Goldberg, you know, the head salesman, called up about it. Well, the next day this Goldberg comes over when I am turnin' in and the boss says he wanted me to take him over to the Astor, and for me to take him; the night-man can wait. Goldberg got in and I started off with him. He sat on one of the little seats so he could talk to me. He says: 'Did you have a party named Klein Wednesday?'

"I says: 'That I couldn't say. Maybe I did. Maybe I didn't.'

"He says: 'I'm the head salesman of the Mongoose Taxi Manufacturing Company. What I say goes with your boss. I can have you fired.'

"I says: 'Well, maybe you can and maybe you can't.'

"He says: 'You rode that man around all day, didn't you?'

"I says: 'Maybe I did and maybe I didn't.'

"He says: 'You took him down to the ———— Apartment-House, didn't you?'

"I says: 'I couldn't say. Maybe I did and maybe I didn't.'

"Then he says: 'Where did you take him from there?'

"I says: 'I couldn't say.'

"He kept at me all the way over to the Astor and then he told me to wait for him. I didn't want to wait for him, so in about half an hour I tells the doorman to find out if he wanted me to wait, and, if not, to get the money. The doorman came back and gave me six dollars and a half. He said the guy didn't want me to wait and asked him how much was on the clock, so he says six dollars and a half. I only had a buck twenty on the clock, so I offered to split it with him, but he didn't want nothin'.

"Well, the next day the boss said that Goldberg had complained that I overcharged him. I said I didn't overcharge him, and the boss says: 'Whaddayu mean you didn't overcharge him?' I wouldn't tell him no more than that I didn't overcharge him. Well, that night this Goldberg was back again and he says: 'You're the fresh taxi-driver that charged me six dollars and a half to take me over to the Astor, and you wouldn't give me no information.'

"I says: 'Did you give me six dollars and a half?'

"'Well, no,' he said, 'I gave it to the doorman.'

"'Well,' I said, 'you'd better talk to the doorman.'

"So him and the boss got in the cab and we goes over to the Astor again. The same doorman was on, you know, that big Irishman. Goldberg says to him: 'Did this man tell you there was six dollars and a half on the clock when he was waiting for me yesterday?'

"The doorman says: 'And who arrh you to be askin' me quistions? Whaht authority have you got?'

"'Well,' says Goldberg, 'I just wanted to know.'

"'Well,' says the doorman, 'if it's any satisfaction to yuh he didn't tell me nothin' whaht was on the clock. I told yuh there was six fifty on the clock and you paid me six fifty, and whaht I done with the six fifty is me own business, and what was on the clock I don't know. End is thir iny more quistions yud like to ask?'

"I drove them back to the garage and the boss says to Goldberg, 'You didn't pay the driver. There's a dollar forty on the clock,' so Goldberg paid me the dollar forty."

SWEET CAPS

I was standing with the Flivver taxi at Sixth Avenue and 4th Street late one night hoping to pick up a couple of stray up-towners too drunk to get home on the subway. I saw a couple coming but they didn't look like business. They weren't drunk, and though the girl was all dressed up, she looked rather thin and worried and the man was little and shabby. They stopped alongside of the cab and looked me over.

The girl said: "Are you working? I may have a job for you in a little while."

"Sure, I'll be here."

She looked across the street, and following her glance I saw a well-dressed man, well lit.

She said to her companion: "That John looks like a live one. Wait here." And she crossed the street.

He took a quick look up and down the street and seemed satisfied and said: "How's business?"

"Tough."

"Nobody's got any money since the war's over."

"I used to make good jack in the shipyards," I said, "but they're all shut down now. I saved some money and bought this hack when things got bad."

"Did you work in the shipyards too? Christ, it was good, wasn't it? I was bucking up before the war, so I got right on rivetin'. What dough we made! Twelve and fifteen cents on shell! I got as much as ten cents on buttonsets in the intercostals."

"Too bad the war didn't last forever, hey?"

"I saved up a big stake but I lost it. I bought a gin-mill and cabaret down here, but yuh can't make no money at it. Yuh have to slip it all as fast as yuh make it, and when yuh can't come across with all they want, they break yuh."

As he talked he kept a sharp lookout. He looked to me to be pretty small for a riveter. Riveting is hard, heavy work, but a few small men make good at it; some of the best I've ever seen. They don't last long at it, though. The strain breaks them down in a few years. I'm big and strong, but my right arm started to go dead and numb after five years with the hammer.

The girl returned looking discouraged. "He's too far gone," she said. "The booze they sell now is sumpin' terrible." Then to him: "Got a cigarette?"

"No, that was the last one."

She rummaged around in her purse for some time and handed him a coin. "You can get a pack of Sweet Caps."

He walked over to the drug-store and she said: "I never saw business so bad. And the cops—my God! I'm just after doing thirty days in Bedford."

I said: "There was a lush here last night you coulda had; too bad you weren't around."

"Think of that. And I didn't get a thing all last night."

"Have you got a room?"

"No; you can't use no room on account of the cops. I always get a taxi. I tell 'em the taxi is five bucks. Of course, if he won't pay the driver that much, I make up the difference myself."

The man returned and they lit their cigarettes. "Here comes one, maybe," the man said. "I'll look him over." He hurried off.

"He's a prince of a fellow. He usta make big money but his health gave out. He ain't strong enough for that shipyard work. He spent a lot on me." Her thin, tense face looked very wistful.

The man came back looking hopeful. "I think you can get that John."

She powdered her nose and hurried off.

He posted himself to watch and said: "She's a great kid. I met her in the cabaret before I bought it. I spent a pile of dough on her. She's made a lot of money. She don't spend no time on 'em at all. Just long enough to get her hooks on that fifteen bucks, and out they go."

The girl returned dejected. "He's no good. Lookin' for charity—them damned school-teachers."

"Here comes a dick," the man said.

"Did he spot us yet?"

"No."

"So long, buddy," they said and hurried off.

II.

HACKMEN

There are all kinds of people driving hacks in New York. There are a lot of gunmen, gorillas, etc., who serve a district leader at election-time and get a certain amount of protection in turn, and who drive taxicabs as a convenient side-line. Most of them are to be found on what are called closed lines; that is, some places where taxicabs stand in line for business at a designated hack-stand, a tough gang will get together and hold the line for themselves and keep outsiders out.

At the other extreme there is a close relative of the late Elbert Hubbard who has been hacking in New York ever since automobiles came in, and he can tell some very good stories if you happen to meet him in one of the Coffee Pots about three o'clock in the morning.

Then there is George Mast. His people have followed the sea for generations. According to his story, he was a captain in the Merchant Marine before the war. During the war he was enrolled in the naval reserve. He had a couple of supply-ships blown out from under him, one right after the other, just off New York Harbor. After the war he was placed in command of a destroyer. One day he received orders by wireless to call in at Bermuda and pick up ten cases of special ammunition. He thought they were funny-looking ammunition-cases, but there was nothing to do but obey orders. When he got into New York Harbor the prohibition officers boarded the ship at quarantine, seized the ten cases of special ammunition, which proved to be a fine assortment of wines and liqueurs from France. The orders apparently were faked by some one.

George was kept out of jail but was retired from the service on part-pay pending an investigation. The papers in the case were supposed to have been forwarded to Washington. The case was never officially investigated.

George is, as he describes himself, "fair, fat, and forty," but he manages to get by driving a taxi, as his part-pay is hardly enough to support his family.

He had to report occasionally to the Naval Reserve office then at Ellis Island. He used to drive the cab down to South Ferry, park the car and put his old tin hack badge in his pocket. The Reserve kept a launch there to ferry people over to the offices. The sailors would remember Mast, salute and man the boat to take him to the Island and for the moment he would be an officer again. Then he would return, put on the badge and go back to hacking.

SOLD THE FORD

I finally decided that I had better sell my Ford taxi and buy a new one, but I thought it a good idea to work for other people and try out the various makes of cars at somebody else's expense before I made a decision as to what to get.

A well-known racketeer, whom we will call Harry, had recently bought five hundred Yellow cabs and had obtained the concession at Grand Central and Penn Station. I went over to their garage on 49th Street and applied for a job. I was sent out with another applicant and a mechanic for a tryout. While I had driven plenty of gear-shift cars years before, I had been driving that one Ford for so long that I had gotten so it was a part of me, like my own hands and feet. I didn't have to think about anything any more. I just thought "stop" and I stopped; I thought "start" and I started. When I took the wheel on the Yellow cab, I was all at sea. I shoved the clutch in expecting the car to go ahead in low. Nothing happened. Then I had to think about shifting gears. When I wanted to give it more gas, I would start scratching around under the steering-wheel for the throttle, and there wasn't any. Then it would occur to me that I had to step on it. So I didn't make a very good showing. The other fellow, however, made out all right, as he had been driving a Shaw previously.

We all went back to the employment office, and the mechanic told the employment-office man something in private and went out. Then the employment manager took down my name and address, license numbers, etc., and gave me a badge, and I was all set to go to work, and he told me to report at the 25th Street garage. Then he turned to the other fellow and said: "I am afraid you haven't had enough experience; you had better go to work for somebody else for a while and then come back."

I saw the employment manager had got us mixed. When the other fellow started in to explain that he had been driving a Yellow right along and knew all about them, the employment manager caught on he had made a mistake, but he didn't want to admit it, so I backed on out the door. I knew the other fellow could come back the next day and get a job if he wanted to, and I also knew that with a few hours' practice I would be perfectly familiar with the Yellow.

WORKING FOR HARRY

I reported at the 25th Street garage that evening ready to go to work on the night-line. It was an interesting bunch of men waiting for the cars to come in.

Harry had been brought up in Hell's Kitchen and had been a taxi-driver, playing the closed lines on the waterfront. When prohibition came along, he got into the bootlegging game and made rapid strides. Possibly his success was due to the fact that he already knew the best of the gunmen and gorillas in New York that were necessary to the business. When he was at the high tide of his success, he bought five hundred Yellow cabs at a crack, got concessions at Grand Central and Penn Station and put all the gorillas in Hell's Kitchen to work driving them. When a West Side gunman got out of Sing Sing, Harry was there to meet him and gave him a job. Most of the drivers were gorillas. The mechanics were gorillas. The checkers were gorillas. The garage superintendent was an ex-heavy-weight prize-fighter of considerable ability. Even the bookkeepers in his office on Times Square were gorillas.

I went very carefully about breaking in on the job. Whenever any one spoke, it had the effect of a threat. One of the drivers asked the superintendent if his car hadn't come in yet, and the superintendent said: "How long have you been working around here? Did you ever get a poke in the nose?" I gave my name and waited quietly until my name was called. I got on the car and got out of the garage very carefully.

I made out very well that night and pulled in about two o'clock in the morning and discovered that we were expected to line up the cars in a certain way outside to drive into the garage. A man at the door would holler out, "All right there," when there was room for another cab to come in.

When you got inside you took gasoline. Then some one said, "Pull up," as though it would be your last moment if you didn't. You then pulled up to the wash-stand and somebody said "Stop." Then a man came around with a box with coins in it which he shook and said: "Put something in the kitty—coffee money for the boys." Nobody dared refuse.

The second night I took a chance and said, "I don't think you boys ought to drink so much coffee; it's bad for your health," and didn't put anything in the kitty. Nothing happened; I think probably because they were so surprised they didn't know what to make of it.

That same night I reported that the rear end didn't sound quite right, for, having driven my own cab, I knew it was better to take care of those things first rather than last. I made the report to the head mechanic. He said: "What? What did you say?" I thought my last moment had come. But I stuck to it, so he jacked the rear end up and gave it a tryout, and great was my relief when he did hear something wrong in it.

One night the superintendent knocked five drivers cold, one right after another, for not pulling up and stopping their cars just to suit him.

There were certain great advantages in working for Harry. For one thing he squashed all summonses. If you got a summons for anything, you turned it into the office and paid no more attention to it. He had to cut that out after a while for his own protection, because the drivers got to going so wild they smashed up all the cars. Along about two o'clock in the morning they used to come west on 49th Street and on 25th Street to the two garages in a more or less steady stream, and crossed Ninth and Tenth Avenues so recklessly that it became customary for the street-car motormen on those avenues to stop at 49th Street and 25th Street while the conductor went ahead to see if the coast was clear.

Now there were lots of closed lines at that time, a closed line being a hack stand held down by a bunch of good fighters who beat up any driver who dares to get a call in that immediate neighborhood. But Harry kept a big Packard car, loaded full of gorillas, standing by the Pennsylvania Hotel, and if a driver got beat up for chiseling a call on any one of those closed lines, he could telephone the office. I was down at South Ferry once when one of his drivers got beat up. In a little while the big Packard appeared. Its occupants came down and each one hired a cab. Then they all drove up somewhere on Greenwich Street. The passengers got out, and from then on you couldn't hear anything but crack, bang, sock. There wasn't anybody able to work the South Ferry line for several days.

After a few of these events, word got passed around and his drivers went unmolested although the buckers who used to work the West Shore Ferry line dared to try cutting tires on his cabs when they worked there. His gorillas came down one night and cleaned them up so thoroughly that their cars were left standing there all the next day. Even their friends were afraid to come down and drive their cars away.

There had been a particularly tough bunch in a line on West 4th Street. One of Harry's drivers picked up a call near there one night, and one of the members of the line threatened him. Harry's man stepped down off his cab and the other fellow hit him. Harry's man knocked the bucker down, and just then a cop came up and was going to put Harry's driver under arrest for assault. The rest of the line rushed up then and told the cop that it was only their own man's fault, that he started it; and they gave their own member warning that if he ever slugged Harry's drivers around there, he could get the hell off the line.

THE BENEVOLENT AUTOCRAT

I went up to the office the next week to get my pay. Another driver there said: "Say, Harry, I want to borrow fifteen dollars."

Harry said: "What do you want with fifteen dollars?"

"I want to get a dress for the wife."

Harry said, "Go on. How can you get a dress for the wife with fifteen dollars?" and pushed him in the face.

The driver said: "Well, I got twenty-five and with fifteen more I can get her a decent dress."

Harry called out to the cashier: "Give him fifteen dollars."

I found that Harry took care of the families of many of the men who were taken sick, sent their sick children to the country, paid their doctor bills. On the other hand, if a driver was caught riding stick up (carrying a passenger with the flag up so the meter wouldn't register the fare), the gorillas would pick him up at night and give him the finest shellacking you ever saw.

In spite of all Harry's generosity and all the beatings that were handed out, the drivers kept on riding stick up. I think they cheated him more than any other cab-owner in town.

One driver had been sick a couple of months and his family had been sick. Harry had supported them, sent them all to the country, kept the family there a long time. And after all that, they got him riding stick up one night. When the gorillas got through with him, he was a sight to behold.

I rode stick up on him myself, made a flat rate to the Bronx one night. I got up to 125th Street when I spotted Harry and the gorillas in the big Packard. I put the flag down real quick and they pulled up along side of me. He says: "Got a good call?"

I said: "Yeah, Bronx."

One of the gorillas got out and looked over the seals on the clock, but he didn't look to see what the clock registered. If he had seen there was only twenty cents on it, my goose would have been cooked.

When he had been running the cabs a year he gave a dinner, for all drivers who had been with him over ten months, at the Pennsylvania Hotel, gave them all gold badges, took them up to the Follies in taxicabs. Under influence of the excitement of the occasion the gorillas socked all the buckers playing the big Pennsylvania Hotel line and put Harry's cabs on the line in their place.

One of the drivers was held up one night by five men, who got about thirty-five dollars off of him and took the cab. He went up to the office and told Harry about it, described the men. Harry made good the money he had lost and told him not to say anything to the police about it.

In the meantime the five men had had an accident with the car, and the police had picked them up, found the driver had no hack license, and knew the car was stolen. The police tried to get Harry and the driver to appear against the five, but he refused, so the police had to turn them loose, which might seem very generous, but the gorillas picked them up about as soon as they got out and beat hell out of them.

FIRED

Harry got up a mutual benefit association for the drivers with dues of fifty cents a week to provide medical service, etc., for the men. We weren't asked to join; the fifty cents was taken out of our pay; so I stopped in at the office and said: "Harry, I'm not interested in this benefit association. I already have my own doctor and own dentist and I would rather not pay the fifty cents a week."

"Well," he said, "that's all right if you don't want it. We'll take your name off the list." Then he said: "Well, I don't know. If we let you out, why then they will all back out. I guess we'll have to let you go, Hazard."

So I said: "Well, all right."

I went over to the cashier to draw my pay in full. After a few minutes Harry came over and said: "Are you married, Hazard?"

"Yes."

"You got any children?"

"Yes, I got one."

He looked very upset, turned to go away, came back again and said: "I'm sorry, Hazard, but I can't help it."

THE MOGUL CHECKERS

In the meantime the Mogul Checker Taxicab Manufacturing Company had sold a lot of taxicabs in New York and they were taking the business away from everybody else. It seemed to me that it would only be a matter of time until there would be so many of them on the streets that they would be cutting each other's throats, or some other cab manufacturer would come out with a new cab, dolled up to catch the public's fickle fancy, and kill them off. These cars sold for three thousand dollars, which was about twice what they were worth from a mechanical standpoint, so I thought it would be better to continue to work for somebody else. I got a job driving for a very unfortunate person who had invested in about sixty Mogul Checkers. We all worked on a percentage basis; that is, the driver got 35 per cent of what the clock registered. Now, it was very easy to make a bargain with a passenger and leave the flag up and keep it up. The only question was how much to turn in to keep from getting fired, so I made it my business to ask the other drivers how much they booked, and found that on the night-line, which I was working, they varied from sixty to a hundred and fifty dollars a week. I noticed the boss kept letting out the tailenders and trying out new men, but the men who turned in better than seventy-five a week were never reached in this process. I was a pretty fair hackman and could have turned in a hundred and twenty, but I thought "Why make the boss a present of forty-five dollars a week?" so I kept close track of it and turned in between seventy-five and eighty dollars. I made cracking good money all that year. I saved on an average of two hundred dollars a month above all living expenses.

THE ADDICT

I picked up a couple one night, and when I got them to their destination they handed me the money but hesitated about getting out. They were rather poor-looking people, about thirty, apparently husband and wife. Then the man stammered a bit and asked me if I knew where a person could go to take the drug cure.

I told him I didn't know but I understood the city ran a kind of place where they put people through a cure. He went on to explain he had got started taking drugs, and the woman chipped in and helped along. I finally got it clear that he had become addicted to drugs through taking stuff for insomnia and now was in a pretty bad way, and it took so much to keep him going, he couldn't make both ends meet any more, and he wanted to get over it some way. I suggested the best thing to do would be to call up the Board of Health and they ought to give him the information. They wanted to know whether, if they would hire me the next morning, I wouldn't attend to it for them, so I said I would.

I called and got the man the next morning. His wife had gone to work apparently. The man looked to be in very bad shape. He said he had been off the stuff for a day and wasn't going to buy any more. I called up the Board of Health. Some girl answered the phone and I told her I wanted to find out about getting a man sent to the city institution for drug addicts. She said: "You will have to come down and see the health commissioner."

I drove down to the Health Department building near City Hall, left the man in the car, went up to the office and told the girl at the desk my business. She told me to sit down and wait; she would tell the commissioner. I sat down and waited and waited. After about an hour the commissioner came out. A woman who had come in in the meantime rushed up and started talking to him. I thought: "Well, I will wait until she gets through instead of raising a disturbance." By and by she got through and the commissioner turned and started to go back into his office. I jumped up and said: "Hey, do you realize I have been waiting over an hour to talk to you?"

"Well, why don't you say what you want?"

So I told him the story.

"Why, we have nothing to do with that business," he explained. "You will have to go see the Board of Narcotic Control."

"Where can I find them?" I asked.

"The girl will look up their address for you."

The girl went through some papers in her desk and told me to go to 148 Bowery, I think. I drove over to the Bowery, went up to a dingy office with a lot of benches around for people to sit on, and a shabby old man at the desk. I told him the story.

He said: "You will have to wait until Mrs. ——————— comes in. She attends to that. Sit down. She will be in pretty soon."

I was getting worried about the poor devil in the cab. He looked pretty bad. I was afraid he might pass out on me, so I went down, helped him up the steps, put him on a bench so I could have him where I could watch him.

We waited and we waited and we waited.

Finally I went up to the desk again and said: "What's the idea? When is this woman going to get in, anyway?"

"Well, I can't make her come in. You will have to be patient. You should realize you are getting all of this service for nothing and appreciate it."

"Yes, and it seems to be worth it."

I sat down and we waited. Finally the woman came in and, after fussing around at her desk for fifteen or twenty minutes, she asked me what I wanted and I told her the story.

She got out a blank and said: "Now, what's your name?"

I told her.

"How long have you been addicted?"

I explained courteously I wasn't addicted.

She continued: "How many members of your family are addicted?"

"My family hasn't got anything to do with it. This fellow wants to take the cure and I want to get him through it."

She said: "Well, you will have to give me all the facts if we are going to do anything for you. We want to do all we can for you but we must know the facts."

I said: "If you want to take down this man's name and have him committed, all right. If you don't, say so."

She grumbled a little bit and wrote the man's name and address down. Then she wanted to know how many members of his family were addicted. I told her I didn't know and I didn't care. Then she went on to explain about how whole families get to taking the stuff, it's so terrible, and so on and so on, what a time they have helping them.

Finally I asked: "Well, what do you do next?"

She looked at her watch and looked at the calendar and said: "It's too late for us to do anything to-day, but maybe if you go up to the other office on 125th Street they will be able to take care of you. You had better go up to see them. I don't think I will be able to do anything for you." She gave me the address on 125th Street.

I lugged the poor devil back to the cab, and we rolled up to 125th Street. I left him in the cab and went up-stairs, told the woman in charge there I had a man I wanted to have committed as a drug addict.

She got out a blank and put down my name and address. I told her I didn't enter into it; the other fellow wanted to be committed. But she insisted on taking it down.

"How long have you been addicted?" she asked.

I told her I wasn't addicted. I had a fellow out in the cab I wanted to get committed.

Finally she put down his name and address. Then she said: "How many other members of your family are addicted to the use of narcotics?"

I explained over again I wasn't addicted, my family had nothing to do with it, and I knew nothing about the other fellow's family.

She said: "Now, are you sure you are not taking it yourself?"

I said: "Well, for God's sake, let's get some action. That poor devil's likely to pass out on me down there."

"Well, we can't do anything about it to-day."

"Can't you send him to a hospital or something?" I asked.

"No," she explained, "the hospitals won't accept anything but ambulance cases, and he isn't an ambulance case as long as he is in a taxicab. No," she continued, "all you can do is to take him down to the other office on the Bowery at nine o'clock Thursday morning. That's the office for receiving."

"Well," I said, "from the way it looks to me this guy will be dead before that time."

"Then you had better get him some of the stuff to tide him over until Thursday morning."

"Where can I get some of it?"

She opened her mouth to answer, then changed her mind. Finally she said: "Well, you ought to be able to get some of it. There are plenty of places."

I went down to see how the passenger was getting along, and he was about gone. He had been throwing up green stuff and had straightened out as stiff as a board in the cab. I couldn't bend his arms or his legs. His face had turned a kind of a yellowish green.

I managed to get out of him where we could get some of the stuff, so I drove over there, got a small bottle of it for five bucks. He took a small shot and commenced to feel better right away, so I took him home and arranged to call for him Thursday morning.

When I got over there for him Thursday morning he was in pretty good shape. The supply had lasted him. I took him down to the Bowery. We waited from nine until about quarter past ten, and the woman hadn't showed up yet. Finally she came in in a great rush and said: "Oh, you are here. Well, now let's see. I have a great deal to attend to to-day. I don't believe I will be able to go over with you, but you can go over there yourself. It's 301 Mott Street, and they will tell you where you go there."

I felt right at home then because 301 Mott Street is the Traffic Court where I have been so often and spent so much good jack.

I drove right over there and asked one of the cops where you go to get a drug addict committed. He gave me the number of the room, and, by jinks! it was the same old room where I had been three or four times previously, where I with a number of others had pleaded guilty and were fined in a bunch.

We went into the room and I said to the clerk: "I have been sent here by the Board of Narcotic Control. I have a man here to take the drug-cure. The Board of Narcotic Control told me ——— ———."

"We don't care anything about that," he interrupted. "All you got to do is give his name. Anybody can come in here and be committed to take the cure that wants to."

That's all there was to it. The man signed his name. The clerk took it into the judge and he signed it. And we were through.

THE DRUNKEN COP

A cop hailed me in Greenwich Village. He had a drunk with him who, he told me, was a cop too, and he wanted me to take him over to some place on Degraw Street, Brooklyn, and that he was all right.

The fellow looked rather like a cop, but I didn't like the looks of it; still, I didn't see any way to get out of it, so I took him. When I got over there he climbed out of the cab in kind of a dazed condition and started walking off without offering to pay the fare, so I walked after him and told him he hadn't paid the fare yet. He opened his coat showing a gun in a yellow holster at his hip, put his hand on it and said: "This is all the fare you'll get."

I went back to the cab and started following him with the cab. When he saw I was following him, he stepped out into the middle of the street and drew the gun. I leaned over in the seat so as to be protected by the cowl and drove the car right at him. He jumped out of the way, but I caught him a glancing blow with the mud-guard and knocked him over and he dropped the gun. I stopped as quickly as possible and backed up to try and get the gun, but he got up and got the gun before I could make it, but I managed to bump him with the rear of the car again. Then he made a run to try to jump on the running-board, but I stepped on the gas fast enough so that he lost his hold and fell again. He got up and started going the other way, so I backed the car, following him that way, which enabled me to use the back part of the car as a shield. When he'd stop and come at me, I'd go into low and shoot ahead a ways. We manœuvred around, up one street and down another for quite a while. Several men came out and advised me to let that guy alone, they knew him, and the best thing I could do was to forget it; but I was working for a company then, and if I didn't get it I would have to pay it out of my own pocket.

He tried grabbing another taxi, but the other drivers saw the situation and got away from him. Then he got a street-car and followed it a ways. Then he gave that up and tried it on foot again. All of this time I had been looking for a cop, but none had showed up. Then I came in sight of a station-house in that precinct, so I thought I would take the chance of losing him, shoot over there and get a cop.

I went in and told the sergeant about it, giving him the name that the cop had addressed him by and the fact that he carried a gun practically unconcealed. The sergeant said: "What do you expect us to do about it?"

I said: "Well, if you don't know what to do about it, I guess that settles it. So long."

He said: "Hold on there now; hold on. Who'd you say this fellow is?"

Again I gave him the name that I had heard the cop address him by and the fact that he carried a gun practically unconcealed.

"Well," he said, "now that's different. I didn't understand before he is supposed to be a cop. I don't think he could have been a cop. That's more reason for us to get after him. There's a lot of guys running around with fake badges. We got a guy the other day with a fake patrolman's badge and a fake captain's badge. You'd better go in and see one of the detectives. There's no use to put a patrolman on this. One of the detectives will bring him in."

I went into the detectives' room and told one of them about it. He had to make out a typewritten report on it. While I was talking to him, I overheard two of the others talking. One said: "I hear there was a guy got bumped off over at Murphy's yesterday. Tough luck."

The other one said: "Yeh, that's just the way it goes. I've been frisking everybody in that place day in and day out, night in and night out, and just when I get a day off something has to happen."

Well, with the report finally made out, one of the detectives went out with me to see if we could find the bird, but after a lot of walking around he decided to give it up. So I never got that two dollars and ten cents.

THE SCOLD

I picked up a woman at the corner of Fordham Road and Webster. She wanted to go to 180th Street and Van Nest Avenue. The cop was holding the traffic on Fordham Road.

She said: "Why don't you go ahead? I don't want to sit here all day. I'm in a hurry."

"I can't. The cop is holding the traffic."

"How's that? There's fifteen cents on the clock already."

"That's the way it works."

"Well, I won't pay it."

"You'll have to."

"Well, I'll get out."

"All right, go ahead, but you'll have to pay me the fifteen cents."

"I'll call an officer," she threatened.

"Fine. That just suits me. There's one right there," and I pointed to one standing about fifteen feet away.

By that time traffic was moving on Fordham Road and she said: "Why don't you go ahead? What's the matter with you? I never saw such a taxi driver."

We had gone about two blocks when she said: "You're going the wrong way. Don't you know where you are going?"

I slowed up. "How do you want to go?"

"Go ahead. Go ahead. Didn't I tell you I'm in a hurry?"

Two blocks farther on she almost screamed: "You're going the wrong way. You're trying to run up a big bill on the clock. I won't pay it."

I put on the brake and said again: "Well, how do you want to go?"

She shouted: "Go ahead, go ahead, I'm in a hurry."

I stepped on the gas again.

She continued: "If you don't know where it is, why didn't you say so?"

"I know where it is." There is hardly any choice as to how to get there and I was going the shortest way and I knew that she must know it.

"How much is the fare going to be?" she asked.

"Oh, about four dollars."

She almost choked. "You're going the wrong way. It shouldn't be more than sixty-five cents."

"Well, I wish you would tell me how you want to go. The more there is on the clock, the more I collect."

"Go on, go on. My people are waiting for me."

We kept this up all the way there.

I had sixty-five cents on the clock and she said: "I'm not going to pay you more than fifty cents. That's all it should be."

"You'll have to pay what's on the clock, and, furthermore, the clock is still running and it will register another nickel pretty soon and you'll have to pay that too."

She finally handed me a dollar and said: "I'm not going to give you any tip."

"That's old stuff. I knew that long ago. It's tip enough to get rid of you."

"You're the worst taxi-driver I ever saw. If it weren't that my people are waiting for me, I wouldn't have ridden in your old cab."

"Don't worry, they can live without you. It's a wonder to me they didn't murder you long ago."

She took a deep breath and was just starting in all over again when I went into low and let the clutch in.

POCKET BOOKS

I am always finding women's pocketbooks in the cab. I brought so many pocketbooks home to my little daughter that she doesn't know what to do with them all. One time I had a couple of cars, so that I had drivers working for me, and they started bringing home pocketbooks to my little girl. We had pocketbooks all over the place.

It's funny they all contained about the same things. The description of one about fits them all: from five to thirty cents; a handkerchief; some sticks of chewing-gum with some portions of sticks, the labels carefully folded over the ends; a mirror; lip-stick; rouge; powder-puff; a rosary; and a small bottle of bichloride-of-mercury tablets. One contained a Christmas list:

Uncle Tom—Necktie.
Father—Socks.
Cousin Jim—Necktie.
Ben—Necktie.
Grandpa—Socks.
Mother—Handkerchiefs.
Aunt Lilly—Handkerchiefs.
Mary—Stockings..
Gene—Stockings.

And one contained a list of words, followed by definitions:

Exquisite—Expensive.
Refined. ———
Hectic—A disease.
Virgin—Young.
Control—When you are experienced.
Selfish—When an old man takes you to a matinée.

Now, I don't know that all women's pocketbooks are like this, but I do know that this is the kind that is left in taxicabs.

ERRORS

I picked up an old fellow the other day who makes an interesting case for those who care for Freud's theory as to errors and for those who are thoroughly acquainted with down-town New York.

He hailed me at Seventh and Greenwich Avenues. He was a middle-aged gentleman, dressed in the style of old, old New York—black cutaway coat, striped trousers, vest with white piping around the neck, a black derby that came near being a high hat. He was just the least bit shabby, and timid.

He said: "Now, I want you to take me to that court on Lafayette Street. Is there a court at No. 57 Lafayette?"

"I don't know. The Criminal Court Building is near there."

"Well, take me down there. It's on Lafayette between Lexington Avenue and 3d Street."

"Hold on," I said. "There isn't any such place."

"Well, it's somewhere in that neighborhood. Maybe it's 3d Street between Irving Place and Lexington Avenue."

My head started to spin. "But there isn't any such place."

"Well," he said, "I'll tell you. We'll go over and inquire at that court on Jefferson Street and Eighth Avenue."

"Wait a minute. That's another one that doesn't exist."

"Why, yes. You must know that place, that big court building there at 6th Street and Tenth Avenue."

"Oh, you must mean Jefferson Market Court, right down here."

"Yes, that's it," he said, but he looked very downhearted, and added: "Greenwich Street and Tenth Avenue."

"All right," I said, and I drove him to Jefferson Market Court, down to the little back door on 10th Street. In a few minutes he came out again, all smiles and bright as a daisy. "I've got it all straight now. I've got it all straight. It's No. 57 Irving Place, right between 3d Street and Lafayette."

"Hold on. I'll go in and ask him myself." As I started in, he trotted along behind me and said: "Maybe it's—" But I didn't give him a chance to give me any more.

To the desk sergeant I said: "Say, Jack, where does this bird want to go?"

He said: "Take him up to the Domestic Relations Court, 57th Street between Third and Lexington."

"Righto."

I started back for the cab, with the old man still trotting along behind me. He said: "Oh, you know him."

"Sure."

I took the old man up to the Domestic Relations Court. He didn't seem to be a bit pleased; rather depressed, if anything. There was eighty cents on the clock. He handed me a dollar, waited for the twenty cents change, and walked off with it.

COMPANIONATE CARS

I have been reading this stuff by Ben Lindsay about sex. I really can't see anything more complicated about the sex business than about the business of buying an automobile.

I like a Packard. I had one that I drove about two hundred and sixty-eight thousand miles. I took care of it, and it never failed me. If I had to get out of a tight place, I could step on the gas, and I knew just what she would do, and she always did it. Owning that Packard to me meant being sure of having the car I liked best, having the exclusive use of it, being sure that no irresponsible person who had no stake in it would put it out of order, being able to take care of it and know that somebody else wouldn't bang it all up. Now if that old Packard could talk I don't imagine that it would resent the fact that I thought I owned it, because it would realize that in so far as I owned it, it also owned me, and I think it would have been rather proud of the fact that it was worth owning.

People who have a lot of money don't have to worry so much about buying a car. If they don't like the first one, they can get a second one; but for ordinary folks it is different.

Maybe a man would like to have a Buick. He feels he would be perfectly satisfied with a Buick. But he hasn't money enough to buy one. Now if he goes and buys a Chevrolet on the instalment plan, what with the expense of keeping up the Chevrolet, he may never get money enough to get a Buick.

Some people like to buy a Chevrolet or a Dodge on the instalment plan. After they have worn the new off of it, they stop making payments and let it be taken away from them.

There are some people of means who like to have a Ford because they don't have to worry about it. If it gets smashed up, they can get another one. A second-hand one can be had for next to nothing.

Then there are some people who prefer to ride in taxis. Of course you can't expect much in a taxi. A lot of them are all battered up. As like as not, the previous passenger has spit all over the floor and scattered cigarette butts around. But you can get one whenever you want it, pay the fare when you get there, and you are through with it. Or, if anything happens to it, you just pay what's on the clock, and get another one.

On the other hand, there are some people that like to have a Packard or a Pierce Arrow or a Rolls-Royce. They would rather get what they want, stick to it, and keep it in good shape. They don't see any fun in riding around in other people's Fords.

Bertrand Russell says jealousy should not be considered a virtue any more, but if you go monkeying around with somebody's Packard for which he has paid good money and thinks highly of, why, you are likely to get a busted nose, and that's all there is to it.

www.ingramcontent.com/pod-product-compliance
Lightning Source LLC
Chambersburg PA
CBHW061255120726
48001CB00001B/312